Thinking Story® Book

SRA MATH
Explorations and Applications

Willoughby
Bereiter
Hilton
Rubinstein

LEVEL 1

Stephen S. Willoughby
Carl Bereiter
Peter Hilton
Joseph H. Rubinstein
Co-author of Thinking Stories **Marlene Scardamalia**

SRA
McGraw-Hill

Columbus, Ohio

A Division of The McGraw·Hill Companies

SRA/McGraw-Hill

A Division of The McGraw·Hill Companies

Send all inquiries to:
SRA/McGraw-Hill
250 Old Wilson Bridge Road, Suite 310
Worthington, OH 43085

ISBN 0-02-674236-5

1 2 3 4 5 6 7 8 9 VHP 01 00 99 98 97

Overview 2

Thinking Stories and Story Problems

What Is a Thinking Story?

A Thinking Story is a kind of "think along." The stories are real stories, designed to be read to students by a teacher. Students, however, do more than simply listen and enjoy. As a story unfolds, students become active participants in the reading, responding to questions that prompt them to think ahead of the characters—to spot what is wrong with something a character has done or said, to predict what is going to happen as a result, or to think of alternative possibilities that the character has not considered.

Nature and Purpose of the Thinking Stories

Thinking Stories are an essential part of SRA's *Math Explorations and Applications* program. As integrated problem solving opportunities they serve the following purposes. The Thinking Stories at this grade level:

- Develop quantitative intelligence—creativity and common sense in the use of mathematics.
- Demonstrate real-world math applications through the various situations the characters encounter.
- Provide models of problem-solving strategies.
- Integrate reading into mathematics.
- Encourage communication in mathematics by discussing the stories and solutions to problems.
- Integrate mathematics by encouraging students to activate problem-solving strategies from a variety of mathematics disciplines, showing that mathematics is not just encountered in isolated lesson practice.

Integrating the Thinking Stories into *Math Explorations and Applications* Lessons

The Thinking Stories intentionally do not neatly introduce or reinforce lesson concepts. Some Thinking Stories apply lesson concepts, some introduce or preteach an upcoming lesson concept, but the majority of stories simply require students to use their mathematical knowledge and logical reasoning, because real life presents us with a variety of problems at the same time. This structure encourages students to integrate mathematics and challenge them to always consider a variety of appropriate mathematical problem-solving strategies instead of routinely following a given problem-solving model. A Thinking Story can introduce a lesson that focuses on different mathematics, encouraging the class to discuss how the mathematics in the two areas compare.

Integrating Mathematics and Language Arts

The Thinking Stories provide a natural connection between Mathematics and Language Arts. The skills that are developed include

Math Skills
- Choosing which operation to use
- Recognizing relevant information
- Recognizing absurd or unreasonable answers
- Deciding when calculation is not necessary
- Recognizing incorrect answers
- Solving realistic measurement problems
- Deciding whether or not a mathematical model is appropriate

Language Arts Skills
- Characterization
- Predicting what will happen in a story
- Making inferences
- Summarizing what has happened in a story
- Listening for details
- Drawing conclusions
- Evaluating information
- Recognizing cause-and-effect relationships

Using the Thinking Stories

Scheduling.

The lesson plans in the Teacher's Guide for this level suggest which of the 20 selections might be appropriate. In general, one story is referenced about every five to eight lessons. Three or four of the Story Problems are also scheduled for days when no stories are read. (See the correlation of the Thinking Story Book and Student Edition lessons on page 126 of this book.)

Students often enjoy hearing their favorite stories and problems a second time, so you might consider scheduling extra sessions with this in mind. Changing the numbers in the problems for the second reading will maintain interest.

Method of presentation.

Read the stories aloud and solve the problems with the class as a whole, unless you have an aide who can work with smaller groups. As you read these stories to students, you might find the following suggestions valuable.

Read each story the way it is written.

You may be accustomed to telling stories in your own words instead of reading them as they are written. This is a good idea if the stories are hard or long, but these Thinking Stories are short and straightforward, and details that seem unimportant may be crucial to the story's outcome. In addition, the particular wording used in a story often gives students clues for shaping their responses.

Use pacing and emphasis to facilitate thinking.

Read each story clearly and slowly. Give students time to think about each question, but not so much time that they forget the point being made. Make it evident to students, with your voice and with eye contact, when you are reading the story and when you are asking them a question. Questions to be asked are called out in blue type. Pause to emphasize when you have completed one point and are shifting to another part of the story.

Stay on track.

Although many of the questions could be discussed at length, it is important to keep a steady pace so that students do not lose the thread of the story. The questions require only brief answers that move students on to the next point in the story. As you read these stories to students, you might find the following suggestions valuable to the next point in the story rather than to a discussion of related issues.

Discuss problems.

Always ask students to communicate how they figured out their answers. Allow debate. Some of the given answers are arguable, and discussions about them can be very productive. For instance, in one problem in the Level 3 book Mr. Muddle is asked how much one half of a 4-kilogram turkey weighs. "Which half?" Mr. Muddle asks. Students are asked if Mr. Muddle's question is foolish. Although most students will think so, the question may be valid. It depends on what one means by half—half the weight, the front half or the back half, and so on. Discussing such problems and answers can stimulate good mathematical thinking.

Think along with students.

Because students have had limited experience with what is involved in clear thinking, model for them things that you want them to do. For example, show them that it is more important to think carefully about the questions than it is to have the right answer immediately. Think aloud about how you would answer a question, then ask students how they went about deciding on their answers.

Use Number Cubes.

Many of the problems call for numerical answers, and Number Cubes are the best way to get all students to participate and respond.

Make students feel good about their answers.

Recognize that most of the questions in these stories have more than one possible answer. Offer praise for even a clearly incorrect answer if the student obviously put some thought into it. Try to show lively interest in all of the students' answers.

Don't encourage snobbery.

The characters in these stories are well aware of one another's imperfections. They are all warm-hearted people who support each other and treat each other with respect. The stories are written so as to convey this attitude to students.

Keep a light touch.

Many of the stories are farcical. Many of the questions call attention to some event or action that is amusing or silly. The stories do not have a serious message, and they should be read and discussed in an appropriate tone.

Adjust to individual and group differences.

Don't expect every student to correctly respond to the problems and the story questions the first time the story is read. Often it will be necessary to repeat problems; many more students will get the point and will reason correctly the second time you read the story. The complexity of the problems varies. You might consider acting out a problem or using manipulatives if students are having unusual difficulty.

The difficulty of the problems and stories increases toward the end of the book. A slower group might not make it to the end, but could benefit from repeating earlier material. A faster group should complete the whole book (even early parts are sufficiently challenging the first time through), without much repetition of the earlier stories and the easier problems.

Although these suggestions may seem a bit directive, if you follow them from the beginning, you will soon discover that they indicate the most natural way of handling the Thinking Stories. If you handle the stories successfully, students will keep asking you to do more because, essentially, that is what Thinking Stories are—something that teachers and students do together.

Developing the Characters in the Thinking Stories

The same characters are used in levels K–6. The main characters in the Thinking Stories are special. Each has a peculiarity in his or her thinking. Students learn to recognize these peculiarities and to try to avoid them in their own thinking as they answer the story questions. The children in each Thinking Story Book are portrayed at the age of the students in the corresponding grade level.

The various characters in the stories and problems have peculiarities that students come to know over time: Mr. Muddle, for example, forgets things; Ferdie often jumps to conclusions without thinking; Mr. Breezy typically gives more information than is needed, and so makes easy problems seem difficult. When students approach a Thinking Story or Story Problem, they know they must be prepared to think and to pay attention to which numbers are important. Students must use a thoughtful approach to problem solving rather than carrying out mechanical, arithmetical operations. The stories and problems are filled with surprises, so students will not fall into a passive rut. And what a good way to prepare students for real life. The thinking problems that some of these characters have are similar to those students often have but may not recognize. In the stories, however, the problems are exaggerated so that students can easily identify them.

The stories are designed to be read to students by an adult. As a story unfolds, students are asked questions that prompt them to think ahead–to spot the problem with what a character has done or said, to anticipate what is going to happen as a result, or to think of other possibilities that the character hasn't considered. The Story Problems that follow the Thinking Story follow this style, but are much shorter.

Main Characters

Mr. Muddle fails to understand the nature of the problems he faces and so applies mathematics inappropriately. In considering Mr. Muddle's absurdities, students learn to appreciate the need for reasonableness in applying mathematical ideas.

Ferdie is impulsive and overconfident. Because of this, he leaps to conclusions without thinking. In the stories in which Ferdie appears, students are encouraged to consider information that he ignores.

Portia, Ferdie's younger sister, is more cautious than her brother. Portia tends to consider and reason before she reaches conclusions. In the stories that include Portia, students get to see what someone who thinks things through might say or do.

Mr. Breezy usually says too much. While trying to be helpful, he confuses people by either by giving irrelevant details or by leaving out important details. In the Mr. Breezy stories, students learn to distinguish the essential information from irrelevant details and to identify which important details he leaves out.

Marcus, Mr. Breezy's son, is another character who thinks things through. He asks questions that help other characters (particularly his father and Ms. Eng) to clarify what they are saying. In the stories in which Marcus appears, students learn to anticipate his questions and are encouraged to think of similar questions on their own.

Cousin Trixie, Ferdie and Portia's fun-loving cousin, enjoys teasing and trying to trick her cousins. Students learn to look twice at what appear to be "bargains."

Manolita thinks that everything "just happens." She never gives much thought to how or why. The stories featuring Manolita encourage students to figure out how things happen as a consequence of some other action or event.

Willy wishes for what he wants to happen, but doesn't do anything about it. In the stories featuring Willy, students are invited to think of ways that he could make things really happen.

Miss Asker asks students questions that help them figure out answers to their problems. Students learn how to break down hard questions into easier ones.

Agatha Misty is a detective who repeatedly jumps to faulty conclusions based on insufficient evidence. Students learn to reassess evidence and the conclusions drawn from it.

Ms. Eng enjoys having a group of people around her. She is very friendly and easy to talk to, however she is often so vague that people have trouble understanding what she is talking about. The stories that include Ms. Eng provide students with opportunities to ask questions that will clarify what she means and to suggest ways that she might say something more clearly.

Units of Measure in the Thinking Stories

Both customary and metric units are used in the Thinking Stories. They are included not to teach the customary or metric system but to help give students a feel for how some of the common units of measure are used in everyday activities. You should know the approximate magnitudes of the units used in the Thinking Stories. The following table is a handy reference.

Length

	Unit	Symbol	Relation to Common Objects or Events
Metric	centimeter	cm	A paper clip is about 1 centimeter wide and 3 centimeters long.
	meter	m	Most classroom doors are about 1 meter wide.
	kilometer	km	It takes about 12 minutes for an adult to walk 1 kilometer.
Customary	inch	in.	A thumb is about 1 inch wide.
	foot	ft	Your math book is about 1 foot long.
	yard	yd	An umbrella is about 1 yard long.
	mile	mi	Four city blocks are about 1 mile long.

Weight

	Unit	Symbol	Relation to Common Objects or Events
Metric	gram	g	A nickel weighs about 5 grams.
	kilogram	kg	A pair of size-10 men's shoes weighs about 1 kilogram.
Customary	ounce	oz	One slice of bread weighs about 1 ounce.
	pound	lb	One loaf of bread weighs about 1 pound.

Volume

	Unit	Symbol	Relation to Common Objects or Events
Metric	liter	L	Four average-size drinking glasses hold about 1 liter of liquid.
Customary	cup	c	A school milk carton holds about 1 cup.
	pint	pt	Two cups equal 1 pint.
	quart	qt	Two pints equal 1 quart.
	gallon	gal	A large can of paint holds about 1 gallon.

How Many Piglets?

Ferdie and Portia could hardly wait for Saturday to come. They were going out to Grandpa's farm to see Martha's babies. Martha is Grandpa's pig, and these were her first babies. Ferdie and Portia had never seen piglets before.

What do you think piglets are? baby pigs

When Saturday came, Ferdie and Portia and their mother got on the bus and rode out to Grandpa's farm. The bus driver let them out right at the gate. Ferdie and Portia ran ahead to the barnyard, where they found Grandpa standing by the pigpen. Martha was standing in the pen, eating—as usual. She didn't even look up. She is not the world's friendliest pig.

What would you have expected the world's friendliest pig to have done? look up

Would she have smiled at Ferdie and Portia? perhaps

All around Martha, running this way and that, were her piglets. Some were pink and some were black, and some were partly pink and partly black.

"Look at them run!" said Ferdie.

"How many piglets are there?" asked Portia.

"Count them yourselves," said Grandpa with a smile, "if you can."

"Of course I can count them," said Ferdie. "That's easy."

Ferdie crouched down beside the pen and counted the piglets as they ran past. He counted, "1, 2, 3, 5, . . ."

"You made a mistake," said Portia.

What mistake did Ferdie make? He skipped 4.

What should he have said? "1, 2, 3, 4, 5, . . ."

"You skipped 4," said Portia.

"All right," said Ferdie, "I'll start again."

This time he didn't skip any numbers. Every time a piglet ran past, he counted. He counted, "1, 2, 3, 4, 5, 6, 7, 8, 9, 10." Then he shouted, "Ten piglets! That's a lot!"

"H'm," said Grandpa, "I didn't think there were that many."

Could Ferdie have made a mistake? How? He may have counted some piglets more than once.

◆ **STORY 1   How Many Piglets?**

"I think you counted some piglets more than once," said Portia. "You counted every time a piglet ran past, and some of them came past more than once. Let me try."

Portia looked into the pen, where the piglets were still running around. She said, "There's a pink one. That's one. There's a black one. That's two. There's a spotted one. That's three. And, oh, there's one with a funny tail. That's four. Martha has four piglets."

"You did that wrong," said Ferdie. "You didn't count all the piglets."

How could Portia have made a mistake? She may have counted only one of each kind of piglet.

"You counted only one pink one," said Ferdie, "and there's more than one pink one. See? And there's more than one black one, too. I don't know how many piglets there are. I wish they'd stand still so we could count them."

"Just wait," said Grandpa. "Maybe they will."

In a little while Martha finished eating and lay down on her side. The piglets stopped running around. They went over to their mother and started feeding.

"Now we can count them," said Portia. "They're all in a row." She counted, "1, 2, 3, 4, 5."

How many piglets did she count? five

"Martha has five piglets!" said Portia.

"That's strange," said Grandpa. "I thought she had more. But you're right, there are only five piglets there."

Just then they heard a sound, "Eee, Eee, Eee," and another piglet that had been off by itself came running across the pen and joined the others.

How many piglets are there now? six

How do you know? There were five piglets before, and another one joined them.

. . . *the end*

◆ **STORY 1** **How Many Piglets?**

Story Problems

1 Portia got a new coat. Before, she had only a brown coat. Now she has a green coat too.
How many coats does Portia have? two

2 Count how many things Marcus did: First he washed his hands. Then he washed his face. Then he brushed his teeth. Then he combed his hair.
How many things did Marcus do? four

3 Ms. Eng had seven rosebushes growing in her backyard. She picked one rose off each bush and gave them all to Willy.
How many roses did Willy get? seven

4 Manolita counted all the fingers on one hand, but she didn't count the thumb.
How many fingers did Manolita count? four

5 "Oh, every wheel on my tricycle is broken," moaned Ferdie.
How many wheels are broken? three

6 Mr. Breezy likes radios. He has a radio in the kitchen. He has a big radio in the living room. He has a clock radio in his bedroom. And he has a radio in his car.
How many radios is that? four

7 Figure out how many horses Grandpa has:
Grandpa has a horse that he rides when he wants
to go horseback riding. He uses the same horse
to pull a wagon when he does farm work. That
same horse, whose name is Arnold, sometimes
pulls a sleigh in the winter. Grandpa takes good
care of Arnold, because Arnold is the only horse
he has.

How many horses does Grandpa have? one

How do you know for sure? because Arnold is his only
horse

8 Loretta the Letter Carrier was delivering the
mail. Count how many letters she delivered: First
she delivered a letter to Mr. Mudancia. Then she
took a letter to Marcus. Then she took a letter to
Ms. Eng. Then she delivered one letter to Ferdie
and one to Portia.

How many letters did Loretta deliver all together?
five

9 Marcus has six jars of paint that he uses to paint
model airplanes. He painted one airplane white.
He painted another airplane red. And he painted
another airplane yellow.

How many jars of paint does Marcus have? six

Willy in the Water

Willy the Wisher is always wishing that things were different, but he doesn't know what to do to make them different. One time he was on vacation at the seashore. Willy had great fun collecting things along the beach and wading in the water, but he kept wishing things were a little different.

Willy had three seashells that he had picked up along the shore. "I love these pearly shells," he said, "but I wish I had four of them instead of three."

What could Willy do to have four shells instead of three? find another shell

Just then Willy happened to notice another shell on the sand. He picked it up. Then he counted his shells again.

How many shells does he have now? four

How do you know? 3 + 1 = 4

"My wish came true," said Willy. "I have four shells now." He also had four shiny white stones that he had found. But that was not how many stones he wanted.

"I wish I had two shiny stones instead of four," said Willy.

What could Willy do to have two stones instead of four? put down two or give away two

Willy couldn't think of any way to have two instead of four, so he kept those four heavy stones with him until they made a hole in his pocket and two of them fell out.

How many stones did Willy have then? two

◆ **STORY 2** **Willy in the Water**

"My wish came true again," said Willy. "I have two shiny white stones now, just the way I wanted." But his wish didn't stay true for long because the other two stones fell out through the hole in his pocket too, and then he didn't have any.

Willy had also found five crab claws, but he wished he had seven.

What could Willy do to have seven crab claws instead of five? find two more

Willy was standing in the water near shore, wishing he had seven crab claws. Then he noticed that the water was about 8 inches deep where he was standing.

How deep is that? Show with your hands. [Demonstrate the correct depth.]

"The water feels good on my ankles," said Willy. "But I wish it were 10 inches deep instead of 8."

What could Willy do about it? wade in deeper

Willy didn't think about wading in deeper. He just stood there in the water, wishing. The tide was going out, so the water kept getting lower and lower. Soon the water wasn't 8 inches deep anymore, but 4 inches, then 2 inches, then 1 inch deep, and finally there wasn't any water around Willy's feet at all.

"Sometimes my wishes come true and sometimes they don't," said Willy.

. . . the end

◆ **STORY 2** **Willy in the Water**

Story Problems

1 Willy's uncle gave him a dog. After a while the dog had three puppies.

How many dogs did Willy have then? four

2 "I'm six years old," said Willy. "When I have my next birthday, I'll be five."

What's wrong with what Willy said? He counted backward instead of forward.

3 Yesterday Ferdie counted six ducks in the pond. Today there are eight ducks.

What could have happened? More ducks arrived; two eggs hatched.

4 Portia had three nickels. She spent two for a pencil.

How many nickels does she have left? one

5 Marcus's mother gave him five grapes. He lost one and ate the rest.

How many grapes did he lose? one

6 Marcus went shopping with his mother and they bought two pairs of shoes. They put the package into the trunk of the car. One shoe slipped out of the box before they got home, but they didn't see it fall.

How many new shoes did they have when they went into the house? three

7 Portia had one pretzel. Mr. Muddle gave her two more, but she gave one of them to Ferdie.

How many pretzels did she have then? two

8 Manolita bought five notebooks at the store. Then she found out that she needed only two, so she took the others back.

How many notebooks did she take back? three

STORY
3

THINKING STORY

Mr. Muddle's Party

Portia and Ferdie stopped by to visit Mr. Muddle. "Mrs. Muddle and I are getting ready to have a party," he said. "You can help me by setting out these funny hats for people to wear."

Portia and Ferdie counted the funny hats. There were four little hats and four big hats. Ferdie said, "I'll bet I can figure out what kind of people will be at your party: four people with little heads and four people with big heads!"

"That's good thinking," said Mr. Muddle. "You almost have it figured out."

"I have an idea," said Portia. "Are you inviting some children and some grown-ups?"

"Yes, I am," said Mr. Muddle.

Can you figure out how many children and how many grown-ups are invited to the party? four children; two or four grown-ups, depending upon whether you count Mr. and Mrs. Muddle

Are you sure? You can't tell for sure how many people are invited just by the number of hats.

"I know! I know!" shouted Ferdie, who always liked to be first with an answer. "Four children and four grown-ups. Who are they?"

"Let me try to remember," said Mr. Muddle. "The grown-ups are Loretta the Letter Carrier, Mr. Mudancia and Mrs. Mudancia, and Mrs. Muddle."

Portia counted the four big hats again. "Mr. Muddle," she said, "there's going to be one grown-up at your party who isn't going to have a funny hat to wear."

Who is that? Mr. Muddle

What did Mr. Muddle forget? to count himself

Mr. Muddle said, "Yes, I forgot about myself. I had an invitation all ready to send myself, but I forgot to mail it."

"Who are the children you're inviting?" Ferdie asked.

"There are Willy and Manolita and some other children," said Mr. Muddle. "I can't remember their names right now."

How many other children should there be? two

How do you know? There are four small hats and Mr. Muddle named only two children.

◆ STORY 3   Mr. Muddle's Party

"There should be two other children," Ferdie said. "I can tell because there are four small hats, and Manolita and Willy and two more make four."

"Are the other two children by any chance a brother and a sister?" Portia asked.

"Yes, I believe they are," said Mr. Muddle.

"And are their names Ferdie and Portia?" asked Ferdie.

"That's right," said Mr. Muddle. "What clever children you are!"

"Oh, good!" said Portia. "We're invited to the party! When is your party, by the way?"

"It's right now," said Mr. Muddle. "I'm sorry. I must have forgotten to send out your invitation. Oh look! I see some guests coming up the sidewalk. You children can help me by standing at the door and handing out funny hats to all the people when they come in."

Do you remember how many funny hats there are? eight

How many big ones? four

How many little ones? four

First Mrs. Mudancia walked in. They gave her a funny clown's hat. Then Mr. Mudancia came in. They gave him a funny hat with a feather in it. He changed it a little by tying the feather in a knot

and said, "Thank you very much." Portia handed Mrs. Muddle a hat too.

How many big hats are left? one

"There's one big hat left," said Portia. "Oh, I know what to do with it. Here, Mr. Muddle." She put the last big funny hat on Mr. Muddle's head, and he went dancing around the room.

Next they heard a child's voice outside, saying, "I wish the door were open so I could come in."

Can you guess who that might be? Willy the Wisher

"That must be Willy the Wisher," said Ferdie. "Come in, Willy." They gave him one of the little hats.

Before long they heard someone walking toward the door singing.

"That sounds like Manolita," said Portia. Sure enough, there was their friend Manolita, standing at the door. They let her in and gave her a little hat.

How many little hats are left? two

Ferdie and Portia waited, but no more children came to the door. "I guess some children that you invited aren't coming," said Ferdie.

Was he right? no

What had he forgotten? to count himself and Portia

"You forgot to count yourselves," said Mr. Muddle. He put the last two funny hats on Ferdie's and Portia's heads, and they all danced around the room.

Suddenly there was a knock at the door. It was Loretta the Letter Carrier. "I hope I'm not too late for the party," she said. "I just finished delivering the mail."

"You're not too late," said Portia, "but something is wrong. There are no hats left. There's no funny hat for you to wear."

Why not? Can anyone remember why there aren't enough hats? Portia put the last hat on Mr. Muddle's head.

"It's all right," said Loretta. "I have my letter carrier's cap, and it will do."

"It will do if we change it a little," said Mr. Mudancia. He turned Loretta's hat around and put the feather from his own hat in it.

"Now we all have funny hats," said Portia, and the party began.

. . . the end

◆ STORY 3   Mr. Muddle's Party

Story Problems

❶ Loretta the Letter Carrier and her husband, Roger, have a baby and a dog. Loretta's mother lives with them.

How many people live in their home? four

❷ Portia gave a party. She invited two girls and two boys. They all came.

How many girls were at the party all together? three

❸ "I had six carrots this morning," said Mr. Muddle. "Then I ate one or two of them—I can't remember which."

How many carrots does he have left? four or five—can't tell

What do you need to know to be sure? how many he ate

❹ Marcus had five apples. Then he ate two apples, only they were someone else's apples, not his own.

How many apples did Marcus have left? five

5 Manolita walked two blocks to the store. Then she walked a block to Marcus's house. After they played for a while, she walked a block to get to her own house.

How far did she walk all together? four blocks

6 Portia planted four beans, but three of them didn't grow.

How many bean plants grew? one

7 Mr. Mudancia wanted to send his brother the smallest letter in the world. He made an envelope just the size of a postage stamp.

How big is that? Show with your fingers. [Demonstrate the correct size.]

He wrote his brother's address on the front of the envelope. Then he pasted a stamp on the front of the envelope and mailed it. His brother never got the letter.

Why not? The stamp covered the address.

8 Willy's father gave him five peanuts. Willy lost one and ate the rest.

How many peanuts did he eat? four

9 When Mr. Muddle got back from a trip, there were seven old newspapers on his porch. He picked up two of them.

How many old newspapers did he leave on his porch? five

THINKING STORY

"It's Not So Easy," Said Mr. Breezy

Mr. Breezy runs a training school for dogs where he teaches them to obey commands and do tricks. People in the community who don't have the time or patience to train their dogs take them to Mr. Breezy. After school and on the weekends, Mr. Breezy's son Marcus helps out at the dog-training school.

"Any jobs for me today?" Marcus asked one Saturday.

"I have some work that needs to be done, but it's not so easy," said Mr. Breezy. "The first job is to figure out how many cans of dog food we have left."

"I'll go to the storeroom and start counting," said Marcus.

"It's not that easy," said Mr. Breezy. "You'll find there are ten cans of dog food there all together. But six of the cans are right-side up. And three cans are upside down. Oh, one can is on its side. Do you think you can handle all those numbers?"

"I don't need to," said Marcus. "I think I know the answer already."

How can Marcus know the answer without going to the storeroom? Mr. Breezy has told him there are ten cans in the storeroom.

How many cans of dog food are there all together? ten

What about the six cans that are right-side up and the three that are upside down and the one that is on its side? It doesn't matter what position they are in.

"There are just ten cans," said Marcus. "I don't have to go to the storeroom because you told me how many at the beginning. It doesn't matter how many are right-side up and upside down and on their sides."

"You're pretty good with numbers," said Mr. Breezy. "I'm proud of you. But here's a problem that's not so easy. You know the chains we use to lead the dogs with when we're teaching them to follow us? Well, I'm trying to figure out how long the chains should be."

"Maybe we can find a book on dog training that will help," said Marcus.

"I've already looked it up in a book," said Mr. Breezy, "but the book gives so many different numbers that there's no way to know which number is best."

Mr. Breezy started to read from the book: "A good chain should weigh about 1 kilogram, should be made of wire $\frac{1}{2}$ centimeter thick, should be 5 meters long, should have about 25 links to the meter, and should be shiny."

"I told you this wouldn't be easy," said Mr. Breezy.

"I think I have the answer already," said Marcus.

How long should each chain be? five meters

What about all the other numbers? They don't matter.

◆ **STORY 4** **"It's Not So Easy," Said Mr. Breezy**

"The book says the chains should be 5 meters long," said Marcus. "The rest of those numbers don't tell how long they should be. They tell you other things about them."

"Spoken like a true Breezy," said Mr. Breezy. "Since you're so good with numbers, maybe you can help with a really tough problem. We need to buy more pens because we can keep only one dog in each pen. We have so many dogs here now that there aren't enough pens for all of them. What is not so easy is to figure out exactly how many new pens we need."

"How many pens do we have now?" Marcus asked.

"I don't know," said Mr. Breezy, "but they're all full."

"Then how many dogs do we have here?" Marcus asked.

"Let me think," said Mr. Breezy. "We have six dogs in the pens out back, four dogs in the pens downstairs, four dogs in the pens upstairs, and three dogs in no pens at all."

"And you want to know how many more pens we need?" Marcus asked.

"I knew you wouldn't think this one is easy," said Mr. Breezy. "So how will we get the answer?"

"But I already have the answer!" said Marcus.

How many more pens do they need? three

How can you tell? Three dogs aren't in any pens.

"We need three more pens," Marcus told his dad, "for the three dogs that aren't in any pens now."

"You make it all sound easy!" exclaimed Mr. Breezy. "What's your secret?"

"My secret," said Marcus, "is to pay attention only to the numbers that matter."

How can you tell what numbers matter? Listen carefully.

. . . the end

◆ **STORY 4** **"It's Not So Easy," Said Mr. Breezy**

Story Problems

❶ Mr. Breezy said, "Our cat, Abigail, had two kittens last year. This year she had three kittens. How many feet does Abigail have all together?"

How many? four, like any other cat

❷ Marcus got up early to mail a letter. Three people saw him while he walked to the mailbox. Nobody saw him while he walked home.

How many people all together saw him walking? three

❸ Ferdie was doing dishes. He had ten plates left to wash. He washed three spoons.

How many plates did he have left to wash? ten

❹ Manolita had three sheets of paper, and she made each sheet into a paper airplane. Two of the planes didn't fly right, so she threw them away. Another one got wet, so she threw it away, too.

How many planes did she have left? zero

5 Ferdie doesn't always pay attention to what people tell him. His mother asked him to get six forks from the kitchen, but he got only five. His mother sent him back for more.

How many more forks did Ferdie have to get? one

6 Mr. Breezy said, "I earned three dollars, then I caught two fish, then I caught a cold, then I lost all my money, then I ate two walnuts. How many dollars do I have left?"

How many? zero

7 Willy lives with his father, his grandmother, his sister, and his brother. Willy and his grandmother were sick on Tuesday, but everyone else felt all right.

How many felt all right on Tuesday? three

8 The teacher said, "Now open your books to page 8." Marcus opened his to page 10.

Should Marcus turn toward the beginning or toward the end of the book? the beginning

STORY
5

THINKING
STORY

Mr. Muddle Goes Shopping

Mr. Muddle invited some friends to his house for lunch. Then he looked in his refrigerator and saw that he didn't have enough food, so he figured out just what he needed to buy and made a list. Then Mr. Muddle left the list on the kitchen table and went to the store.

"Good morning, Mr. Muddle," said Mrs. Frazier, who owns the grocery store. "What do you need today?"

"Well," said Mr. Muddle, "I need eggs, apples, oranges, and tomatoes."

"How many eggs?" asked Mrs. Frazier.

"I don't know for sure," said Mr. Muddle.

Why isn't Mr. Muddle sure how many eggs he needs? He forgot his list.

"Oh, I see you forgot your list again," said Mrs. Frazier. "Can you remember *about* how many eggs you need?"

"All I can remember," said Mr. Muddle, "is that it is one more than five."

Can you figure out how many eggs Mr. Muddle needs? six

"I believe you need six eggs," said Mrs. Frazier. She gave Mr. Muddle a half-carton of eggs with six eggs in it.

"Now," said Mrs. Frazier, "how many apples do you need?"

"I can't remember that either," said Mr. Muddle, "but I know it is less than ten."

Can Mrs. Frazier be sure exactly how many apples Mr. Muddle needs? Why not? No; Mr. Muddle hasn't told her enough.

"You haven't told me enough, Mr. Muddle," said Mrs. Frazier. "There are lots of numbers that are less than 10. Is it eight apples you need?"

"No," said Mr. Muddle. "It is one less than eight."

Now can Mrs. Frazier be sure? yes

How many apples does Mr. Muddle need? seven

◆ STORY 5   Mr. Muddle Goes Shopping

"You need seven apples," said Mrs. Frazier. "Here they are. Now, how many oranges do you need?"

"I don't know," said Mr. Muddle, "but it's the same as the number of fingers I have on one hand."

How many oranges does Mr. Muddle need? five

How do you know? Five is the same as the number of fingers on one hand.

"That was easy," said Mrs. Frazier. "Here are your five oranges, one for each finger. Now all we need to know is how many tomatoes you need."

"I really can't remember that," said Mr. Muddle. "All I know is that I'm going to use eight tomatoes for lunch, and I don't have that many tomatoes in my refrigerator."

Can Mrs. Frazier be sure how many tomatoes Mr. Muddle needs to buy? no

What else does she need to know? how many tomatoes are in his refrigerator

"I can't be sure how many you need," said Mrs. Frazier. "If you have a lot of tomatoes in your refrigerator already, then you won't need to buy very many. I know you want to have eight tomatoes all together. It would help if I knew how many tomatoes you have in your refrigerator right now."

"Oh, I can tell you that," said Mr. Muddle. "I don't have any tomatoes at home."

Now can you figure out how many tomatoes Mr. Muddle needs to buy? Yes. He needs to buy eight tomatoes.

"I think I can figure that one out," said Mrs. Frazier. "You need eight tomatoes and you don't have any, so you need to buy all eight tomatoes. Well, here they are. I hope we didn't forget anything."

"l don't think we did," said Mr. Muddle. "I can't remember anything we forgot."

. . . the end

◆ **STORY 5** **Mr. Muddle Goes Shopping**

Story Problems

❶ Somebody asked Mr. Muddle, "How many children do you have?" "Well, I'll tell you this," said Mr. Muddle, "it's one fewer than the number of noses I have."

How many children does Mr. Muddle have? zero

How did you figure it out? He has one nose, and $1 - 1 = 0$.

❷ "How old are you?" somebody asked Portia. Portia pointed to her ears, her eyes, her nose, and her mouth. "Count them all up," she said. "That's how old I am."

How old is she? six

❸ Yesterday Ferdie borrowed three pennies from Manolita. Today he gave back two pennies.

Does he still owe Manolita any money? yes

How much? 1¢

❹ The Engs' dog, Muffin, buried two bones, then three cans, then one potato, then two bones, then three old newspapers.

How many bones did Muffin bury all together? four

❺ "We've had bad weather for five days," said Loretta the Letter Carrier. "It rained for two days and snowed the rest of the time."

How many days did it snow? three

6 Willy has a rabbit that is worth one dollar. His brother has two rabbits just like it.

How much are his brother's rabbits worth all together? $2

7 Portia ate two apples and an orange after lunch. Later she ate another apple.

How many oranges did she eat all together? one

8 The puddle in Willy's backyard is 4 feet wide. It used to be 5 feet wide.

What could have happened? It might have dried up or drained.

9 Ferdie and Portia each have a pillow stuffed with feathers. Portia thinks her pillow has more feathers in it, and Ferdie thinks his does. "I know how we can find out," said Portia. "Let's open up our pillows and count all the feathers."

Is that a good idea? Why not? too many feathers to count; they'd blow all over and the pillows would be ruined

Can you think of a better way for them to tell without counting? by weighing the pillows or measuring their thicknesses, for instance

STORY
6

THINKING
STORY

Exactly What to Do

"It's time to walk the dogs," said Mr. Breezy.

That was a job Marcus sometimes did at his dad's training school for dogs. He took the dogs to a small park that was right next to the school.

"How many times should I walk around the park with the dogs tonight?" Marcus asked.

"That's not so easy to figure out," said Mr. Breezy. "But here's exactly what you'll need to do. First pat each dog on the head two times. Then walk the dogs around the park two times. Then stop at the drinking fountain for three drinks of water. Then walk the dogs around the park one time. Then say 'Nice doggie' two times. Then put the dogs back into their pens."

"I see what you mean," said Marcus. "That's not so easy, but at least now I know how many times to walk around the park."

How many times does Marcus need to walk the dogs around the park? Three; [Repeat Mr. Breezy's instructions if necessary.]

Marcus figured out that his dad wanted him to walk the dogs around the park three times. He knew that patting the dogs on their heads and saying "Nice doggie, nice doggie" wouldn't help him figure out how far to walk.

When Marcus brought the dogs back from their walk, he remembered that one dog, Bowser, hadn't been fed yet. "How much dog food should I give Bowser?" Marcus asked.

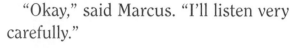

◆ **STORY 6   Exactly What to Do**

"That question's not so easy," said Mr. Breezy. "Bowser's pretty fussy about how much he eats, so you have to do everything exactly right."

Does that help Marcus to know how much food to give Bowser? no

"Okay," said Marcus. "I'll listen very carefully."

"Here's exactly what to do," said Mr. Breezy. "Take two spoons. Then put one spoon into the sink. Then take the other spoon and put two spoonfuls of dog food into the bowl. Then say 'Good old Bowser!' three times. Then put two spoonfuls of water onto the flowers on the windowsill. Then mop the floor. Then put another spoonful of dog food into the bowl, and then another one. Then watch the news on television. Then put one more spoonful of water onto the flowers."

"Now I know exactly how much food to give Bowser," said Marcus.

Do you know how much food Bowser should get? four spoonfuls

Marcus did everything exactly the way his dad had told him to. It took almost an hour until he finished feeding Bowser.

"You're quick at figuring things out," said Mr. Breezy, "but you don't seem to move very fast. How could it take you almost an hour to feed a dog four spoonfuls of dog food?"

Why did it take so long? Marcus had other things to do.

What other things did Marcus have to do? He had to put one spoon in the sink, say "Good old Bowser!" three times, put two spoonfuls of water onto the flowers on the window sill, mop the floor, watch the news on television, and put one more spoonful of water onto the flowers.

. . . the end

◆ **STORY 6** **Exactly What to Do**

Story Problems

❶ "It's not so easy," Mr. Breezy told Marcus, "but here's what you'll need to do: The first thing is to put on your shoes. The third thing is to bring in the newspaper. The fourth thing is to pet the dog."

What did Mr. Breezy forget? the second thing

❷ Yesterday it rained for two hours before lunch. Then the sun came out for a while. Then it rained for another hour.

How long did it rain all together? three hours

❸ The Tates have three children. Two have gone on a bus to visit their grandmother. One is away at college.

How many children are at home? zero

❹ Mr. Muddle has five fishbowls. Each bowl has zero fish in it.

How many fish does Mr. Muddle have all together? zero

❺ Mr. Breezy made up this riddle: "I'm thinking of a number that's less than seven and greater than two and less than four and greater than one."

Can you figure out what number it is? three

How can you be sure? It's the only number that's greater than two and less than four.

6 Mr. Breezy, Mr. Eng, and Mr. Mudancia were having coffee at Mr. Muddle's. "I'm going to have a piece of pie," said Mr. Muddle. "How about the rest of you?"

"Yes, thank you," said Mr. Breezy.

"Yes, thanks," said Mr. Eng.

"No, thank you," said Mr. Mudancia. "I'm on a diet."

How many pieces of pie should Mr. Muddle serve? three

7 Mr. Mudancia had a wooden chair with four legs. Then he changed it a little. He took a broomstick and cut it in half. He put each half under the chair for an extra leg.

Picture that chair in your mind. How many legs does it have? six

8 Marcus's mother likes rings. Marcus wants to buy her a ring for her birthday. He wants to be sure it's the right size for her finger, but he can't ask her—he wants it to be a surprise.

Think of ways that Marcus could find out what size ring to buy. Measure one of her rings; make a clay model of it; find a stick that fits into it; try it on his thumb.

9 Mr. Breezy said, "Our cabin was full of flies. I swatted six flies with a newspaper. Then I swatted four more with a magazine. Then I got two of them with a dust cloth and three of them with a bath towel. But there were still a lot of flies left."

What worked best for swatting flies—paper or cloth? paper [Repeat the problem if necessary.]

STORY
7

THINKING
STORY

Manolita's Amazing Number Machine

Ever since Manolita saw the super-computer her mother works with, she often dreams about amazing machines. One night in a dream she came upon a big machine with an opening on the top and a door at the bottom. Manolita had no idea what kind of machine it was, but she thought she might find out by putting some money in it. She put a penny into the top of the machine. The machine went "Glinka-Glinka" and out popped three pennies at the bottom.

Then Manolita put in a pencil. The machine went "Glinka-Glinka" again and out popped three pencils! "This is great!" chirped Manolita. "I wonder what will happen if I put in three pencils."

What do you think will happen? Offer praise to students who say five (+2) or nine (x3) pencils will come out.

Manolita dropped in the three pencils. The machine went "Glinka-Glinka" and out came five pencils. Manolita had thought there might be a few more than that, but she was happy to have five pencils anyway. "I have a great idea!" she said. "I'll put all my money into the machine, and maybe it will give me back so much money that I'll be rich."

She opened her piggy bank and took out all her money. There were 30 pennies. Eagerly she put all 30 pennies into the top of the machine.

How many pennies do you think she will get back? 32

Would it have been better for Manolita to put in the pennies one at a time? yes

◆ **STORY 7   Manolita's Amazing Number Machine**

The machine went "Glinka-Glinka" and out came 32 pennies. Manolita thought the machine might have made a mistake. She put the 32 pennies in, the machine went you-know-what again, and out came 34 pennies. Manolita tried it once more. She put in the 34 pennies, and this time the machine gave back 36 pennies. "I think I have it figured out," said Manolita as she put in the 36 pennies.

How many pennies will she get back this time? 38

The machine went "Glinka-Glinka" and out came a heap of pennies. Manolita counted them. "Just as I thought," she said. "When I put in 36 pennies, the machine gave me back 38. Every time I put some things into the machine I get more."

How many more? two

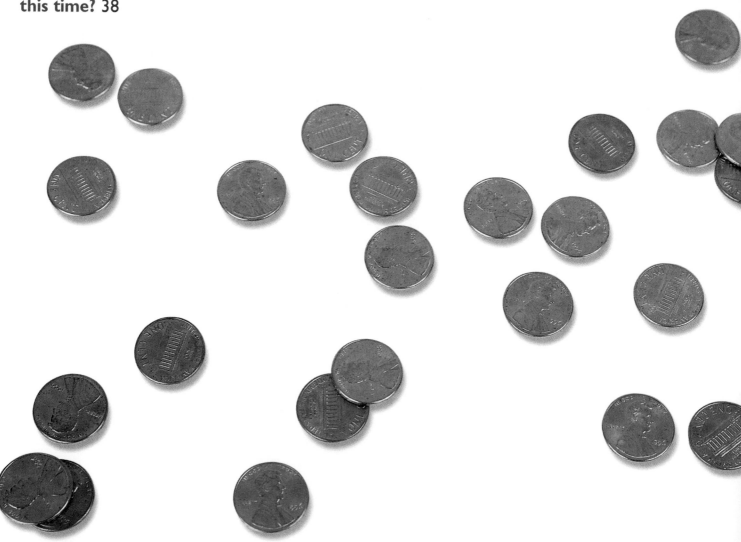

"I always get two more than I put in," said Manolita. "So, if I put my two turtles into the machine . . .

What will happen? She'll get four turtles.

Manolita did it; and, sure enough, the machine gave back four turtles. Then Manolita took five of her mother's silver spoons and put them into the machine.

How many silver spoons will she get back? seven

The machine gave back seven silver spoons, two more than Manolita had put in. Then Manolita had a wild idea: "What if I climb into the machine myself?"

What do you think will happen? Perhaps two more Manolitas will come out.

We'll never know for sure because Manolita woke up just as she was starting to climb into the Amazing Number Machine.

. . . *the end*

◆ **STORY 7**   Manolita's Amazing Number Machine

Story Problems

1 Another night Manolita dreamed about a money-changing machine. If you put in a dime, it gave back 11 pennies. If you put in a quarter, it gave back 26 pennies.

How many pennies would it give back if you put in a nickel? six

2 Manolita put ten potatoes into a different kind of change machine. She got back eight potatoes. She put in five books and got back three.

What was the machine doing? subtracting two

3 Willy had six marbles. He lost half of them.

How many marbles did he lose? three

4 Ferdie had one dollar. He bought two bagels.

How much money did he have left? can't tell

What do you need to know before you can tell? the cost of a bagel

5 "That tree is two years older than I am," said Mr. Burns, "and I am 40 years old."

How old is the tree? 42

6 Portia lives on the second floor of an apartment building. Her friend Janet lives on the fourth floor.

How many floors up does Portia have to go to visit Janet? two

How many floors up does Janet have to go to visit Portia? She doesn't go up; she goes down two floors.

7 Willy had a frog that could jump very high. One day it was hopping across the lawn. Suddenly it jumped 2 feet straight up. Then it fell back down to the lawn.
How far did it fall? 2 feet

8 Marcus invited five boys to his party. They all came.
How many boys were at the party all together? six

9 Ferdie is usually 4 inches taller than Portia, but now Portia is standing on a box that is 4 inches high. They are both standing against the wall.
Who comes up higher on the wall–Ferdie or Portia?
Neither, they are the same.
How do you know? If Ferdie is taller than Portia by 4 inches, but she is standing on a box that is 4 inches high, then they are the same height.

10 Ms. Eng counted 22 roses on her rose bush in the morning. In the afternoon, there were 18.
What could have happened? Some fell off; some were picked.

11 Mrs. Mudancia had a mirror with four lightbulbs on one side and four on the other. One day Mr. Mudancia changed it a little. He took out two of the lightbulbs.
How many lightbulbs does it have now? six

STORY
8

THINKING STORY

Silly Dreamer

Willy the Wisher is always wishing things were different. One day when he didn't have anything better to do, Willy sprawled out on his bed and started looking around his room. His eyes fell upon a stack of library books on his desk. He counted four books in the stack. "I wish there were twice as many books in that stack," said Willy.

How many books did Willy wish were in the stack? eight

Next Willy began staring at the ceiling where he had hung three baseball posters. "I wish I had seven more posters," said Willy, who was very fond of baseball.

How many posters did Willy wish he had? ten

Next to Willy's bed is a chair, which that particular day had four T-shirts piled on it. Willy has never been a child who likes to put away his clothes. "I wish there were four fewer shirts on that chair," said Willy.

How many shirts would there be on the chair if Willy's wish came true? zero

Willy's attention was then drawn to a large wooden bookcase, where he proudly displays his rock collection. He especially likes shiny rocks, but he has only three good ones. "I wish I had five more shiny rocks," said Willy.

How many shiny rocks did Willy wish to have? eight

◆ **STORY 8**   **Silly Dreamer**

Just for fun, Willy likes to scrunch up pieces of paper into balls and toss them into his wastepaper basket. Willy noticed there were five paper balls on the floor near his wastepaper basket. "I wish there were four fewer balls of paper on the floor," said Willy.

How many paper balls would there be on the floor if his wish came true? one

Trying to get more comfortable, Willy stretched out on his back and placed his hands behind his head. This gave him a view of his entire bedroom, which is 10 feet wide and 13 feet long. "I wish my room were 2 feet wider and 3 feet longer," said Willy.

What would be the size of Willy's room if his wishes came true? 12 feet wide and 16 feet long

Just then Willy's mother poked her head into Willy's doorway. "Hey, silly dreamer," she said. "How about dreaming up a way to get your chores done before dinner?"

"OK, Mom," said Willy, pulling himself up to a sitting position. "Now there's a wish I'd *really* like to come true," he thought to himself.

. . . the end

◆ **STORY 8** **Silly Dreamer**

Story Problems

❶ "I'm thinking of a number that's less than 6 and greater than 7," said Ferdie.

What number could it be? None—but a child might suggest 6 1/2.

What's wrong with what Ferdie said? A number cannot be less than 6 but greater than 7.

❷ "This is the third time today that I've asked you to hang up your coat," said Marcus's father.

What will the next time be? fourth

❸ "How old are you?" somebody asked Ferdie. Ferdie held up a cube. "One year for each side of this cube, plus one extra year," he said.

How old is Ferdie? seven; [Allow students to use Number Cubes to solve the problem.]

❹ Ms. Eng took five friends for a ride in her new minivan. The next day she took five more friends for a ride.

How many friends did she take for a ride all together? ten

⑤ Poor Ferdie dropped a nickel down the drain and couldn't reach it. A boy with long arms came along and said, "I'll get it for you if you'll pay me 10 cents."

Should Ferdie pay him? no

Why would it be a silly thing to do? It would cost more than the nickel he lost.

⑥ Manolita went fishing with Ms. Eng. Manolita caught one fish at two o'clock, one at three o'clock, and one at four o'clock.

How many fish did she catch all together? three

⑦ Portia can jump 3 feet. Ferdie can jump 6 inches farther.

How far can Portia jump? 3 feet

⑧ When Mrs. Mudancia stretches as far as she can, she can reach 2 yards up.

If she stands on a stepstool 1 yard high, how high can she reach? 3 yards

⑨ Remember, Mrs. Mudancia can reach 2 yards up if she stretches. She wants to paint a windowsill that is 4 yards high.

How high a platform will she need to stand on? 2 yards

Mr. Mudancia Builds a Better Tree

One day Mr. Mudancia looked out at the tree in his backyard. "I've changed everything else around this house," he said, "but that tree is still the same. It's a nice tree, but I think I'll change it a little."

He measured the tree and found it was 6 yards tall. He changed it so it was 5 yards tall.

How could he do that? by cutting off the top, for example

How much would he have to cut off the top? 1 yard

What would the tree look like afterward? a little flat

Mr. Mudancia took a saw and cut off the top part of the tree so that the tree was a yard shorter. "H'm," he said, "a little flat, but at least it's different." Then he noticed that the tree had eight branches on one side and ten branches on the other side. He wanted the tree to have the same number of branches on both sides, so he changed it a little.

How could he make the tree have the same number of branches on both sides? by cutting two branches off one side

Mr. Mudancia chopped off one branch from the side of the tree that had ten branches. Then he nailed that branch to the side of the tree that had eight branches.

How many branches are on each side of the tree now? nine

Is there anything wrong with this way of changing the tree? The branch will die.

Mr. Mudancia was happy to find that there were now nine branches on one side of the tree and nine branches on the other side, although one branch looked a bit strange. Then he counted 18 apples growing on the tree. "Not bad," he said, "but I'd like it to have 20 apples."

What could he do? He will need to get more apples somewhere else.

How many more apples does he need? two

◆ STORY 9   Mr. Mudancia Builds a Better Tree

He bought two apples at the store and then tied them to the tree with string. "The tree is almost perfect now," he said. "All it needs is a flag at the top." He took a pole about 1 yard long and put it on top of the tree. Then he attached a flag with a big *M* on it.

How high was the tree before he added the flag? 5 yards

How high is the whole thing now? about 6 yards

Tell all you know about what the tree looks like. Do you think it is really better than it was before? The tree has a flat top. It is 5 yards high with a 1 yard flag pole on top. There are nine branches on each side of the tree, but one of the branches has been nailed on. There are 20 apples on the tree, two of which are tied on with string.

. . . the end

◆ STORY 9   Mr. Mudancia Builds a Better Tree

Story Problems

1 Willy had a favorite branch on the tree in his backyard. One day he counted the leaves on the branch and found there were 12. A few days later there were 15.

Which season of the year do you think it was? spring

Why? There aren't very many leaves on the tree, but the number of leaves is growing.

2 "Whenever I lose a tooth," said Willy, "I find ten cents under my pillow the next morning. But today I found only nine cents and a note that said 'You'll get the rest tomorrow.'"

How much money will Willy find under his pillow tomorrow? 1¢

3 Mr. Mudancia changed his bed a little by putting new legs on it. Now, when he lies on the bed, his head is higher than his feet.

What can you figure out about the legs on the bed? The legs at the top of the bed are longer than those at the other end.

4 Mr. Muddle's house used to be 10 yards high. Now it is 9 yards high.

What could have happened? It's sinking or settling; the chimney fell off.

5 Poor Willy is carrying a heavy load. He was already carrying three books, and then Ferdie got him to carry his books too.

How many books is Willy carrying all together? can't tell

What do you need to know before you can tell? how many books Ferdie gave him

6 Willy lives three blocks from school. Ferdie lives one block farther away from school than Willy does.

How far from school does Ferdie live? four blocks

7 Portia had six pennies. She put one in her pocket, then one fell down a sewer. She noticed one penny was three years old.

How many pennies does she have left? five

8 "Last night I went to bed at nine o'clock," said Ferdie. "Tonight I have to go to bed by ten."

How much later does Ferdie get to stay up tonight? one hour

9 Karen is about 3 feet tall. Her uncle is about twice as tall.

About how many feet tall is Karen's uncle? six

10 Manolita and Portia sat on one side of the seesaw, while Virginia sat on the other. They balanced nicely.

Who is the heaviest? Virginia

How do you know? She balances the weight of the other two.

Marcus Builds a Birdhouse

Marcus and Mr. Muddle built a big, beautiful birdhouse. They made it out of a wooden box. They put a roof on it, painted it green, and set it on a post in the backyard. Some big birds came and looked at it, but they didn't go in. "No wonder," said Marcus's mother. "You forgot something important."

What do you think Marcus forgot? to make a hole so the birds could get in

"I see what it is," said Marcus. "We forgot to make a hole in the front of the birdhouse so the birds can get in!"

Marcus went down the street to Mr. Muddle's store and told him the problem. Mr. Muddle brought a drill to Marcus's house. With it Mr. Muddle drilled a hole about 1 inch wide in the front of Marcus's birdhouse.

How wide is 1 inch? Show with your fingers. [Demonstrate the correct width.]

The next day the big birds came and looked at Marcus's birdhouse again, but they still didn't go in.

Why not? The hole is only 1 inch in diameter.

"I'm afraid that hole is too small for those big birds," said Marcus's mother. "What you need is a hole that's the same size as the birds."

Marcus went back to Mr. Muddle and told him he needed something to cut a bigger hole in his birdhouse. "Exactly how big?" asked Mrs. Muddle, who was helping out her husband that day.

"I don't know exactly," said Marcus. "It should be a sort of bird-size hole."

"Birds come in all different sizes," said Mr. Muddle. "You'll have to find out how wide the birds are before you'll know how wide a hole to make."

Marcus took a ruler and went out and tried to measure the birds.

Do you think that worked? Why not? Probably not; the birds would just fly away.

◆ STORY 10 Marcus Builds a Birdhouse

The birds were friendly and Marcus had no trouble getting close to them; but every time he reached out to put the ruler against one, it flew away.

Marcus's friend Portia said, "I have an idea. Why don't you find a picture of that kind of bird in a book and measure the picture? The picture won't fly away."

Does that sound like a good idea? Why not? The picture might not be the same size as the bird.

Marcus looked through a bird book until he found a picture of a bird that looked just like the birds that had come to his birdhouse. He measured the picture with his ruler and found that the bird was 1 inch long. "That can't be right," Marcus said.

How did Marcus know that couldn't be the right size? If birds are wider than 1 inch, they surely must be longer.

Marcus took the bird book over to the Muddles' house and showed the picture to them. "Here's the kind of bird it is," said Marcus, "but I can't find out what size it is."

"Oh, I know that kind of bird," said Mrs. Muddle. "There are some birds like that building a nest in our house, up in the attic."

"How do they get into your attic?" Marcus asked.

"There's a hole in the roof just big enough for them to get through," said Mr. Muddle. "We were going to fix it someday, but now I guess we won't."

Does that give you an idea? How could you find out what size hole to make in the birdhouse? by measuring the hole in the Muddles' roof

Marcus hurried up to the Muddles' attic, stood on some sturdy boxes, and measured the hole in the roof. It was just 2 inches wide.

How wide is that? Show with your fingers. [Demonstrate.]

The Muddles didn't have a drill 2 inches wide, but they had a little saw that would do the job. Mrs. Muddle and Marcus cut a neat hole 2 inches wide in the front of Marcus's birdhouse. Before long the birds came back. This time they went inside and came out again and soon began bringing grass, string, and feathers to put inside their new home.

. . . the end

◆ **STORY 10   Marcus Builds a Birdhouse**

Story Problems

❶ "I want to measure the inside of this box," said Marcus, "but it's too small to get the ruler inside."

Can you think of some ways to measure the inside of the box? by using string or a paper strip; by measuring the outside of the box

❷ Willy has a piggy bank with different slots for pennies and nickels. Nickels will not fit into the slot for pennies.

Do you think a penny will fit into the slot for nickels? yes

Why? A penny is smaller than a nickel.

❸ Ms. Eng likes rings, so Mr. Eng bought her a ring for every finger on each hand, including the thumbs.

How many rings did he buy her? ten

❹ Manolita had two dimes. She spent one for a red balloon.

How many dimes did she have left? one

5 Portia has nine baseball cards. Willy has one more than that.

How many baseball cards does Willy have? ten

6 Marcus walked five blocks to school. After school he went home on the bus.

How many blocks did he walk all together? five

7 For dinner Mr. Muddle ate two ears of sweet corn and two sausages. He left the corncobs on his plate.

How many corncobs were on the plate? two

8 A mother duck had four ducklings. When she wanted to go somewhere, she quacked so the ducklings would all follow her. One day when she quacked, one duckling came out of the barn and two came out from under a bush. After a while another duckling came out of a pile of straw.

How many ducklings were still lost? zero

9 Ferdie lives in an apartment on the second floor. One day he looked out his window and said, "I wonder how to measure how far it is to the ground."

How could he find out? Can you think of ways to measure how far it is? Drop a string, then measure it; measure from the first floor to the ground, then double the measure; ask somebody who knows; estimate on the basis of a known height nearby.

STORY **11**

THINKING STORY

Ferdie Buys a Snack

One day when Ferdie was walking down the street he got very hungry. "I guess I forgot to eat breakfast today," he said, "and lunch too." Just then he saw a snack machine with his favorite crackers in it, Crispy Cracklers. He looked closely. The price for the Crispy Cracklers was 10¢.

Ferdie looked through his pockets. He found six cents in one pocket, two cents in another pocket, and one cent in another.

How much money did he find? 9¢

Is that enough? no

No, he got his ten pennies back. He tried again and the same thing happened. Just then Mr. Mudancia came along.

"What's your trouble, Ferdie?" he asked.

Ferdie said, "This machine doesn't work, and I'm starving to death."

Mr. Mudancia looked at the machine. He read a little sign. "It says to use nickels, dimes, or quarters. You're using pennies."

"All I have is pennies," Ferdie said sadly. "I guess I'll have to go hungry."

Is there anything else Ferdie can do? He can trade his pennies for two nickels or a dime.

He counted and found he had only nine cents. Then he reached down in his shoe and found another penny.

Is a penny the same as a cent? yes

How much money does he have now? 10¢

Ferdie put his ten pennies into the machine. The machine went "Clatter-clatter-clink-clink."

Did he get the Crispy Cracklers? no

◆ STORY 11 Ferdie Buys a Snack

"You can trade your ten pennies for something that will work in the machine," said Mr. Mudancia.

Could Ferdie trade his ten pennies for a quarter? Why not? No, ten pennies are not equal to a quarter.

"A great idea!" said Ferdie. "I believe a dime is worth ten cents. Do you have a dime?"

"No," said Mr. Mudancia. " I only have nickels."

Should Ferdie trade his ten pennies for a nickel? Why not? No, ten pennies are worth two nickels.

"A nickel is worth five cents," said Ferdie. "I'll give you five pennies and you give me a nickel. Is that a fair trade?"

"Yes," said Mr. Mudancia, "that's a fair trade." Ferdie gave him five pennies and Mr. Mudancia gave Ferdie a nickel.

Ferdie put the nickel into the machine, but it still wouldn't give him the Crispy Cracklers. "This machine still doesn't work," he said. "I put in a nickel just as it said, but it didn't give me anything."

Did Ferdie put enough money into the machine? no

How much does a pack of Crispy Cracklers cost? 10¢

How many cents is a nickel? five

How many nickels does Ferdie need? two

"A nickel is only five cents," said Mr. Mudancia. "Crispy Cracklers cost ten cents. You have to put in two nickels."

"But I have only one nickel," said Ferdie.

How could Ferdie get another nickel? trade his five pennies for one nickel

"You still have five more pennies," said Mr. Mudancia. "If you give them to me, I'll give you another nickel."

Ferdie gave Mr. Mudancia the five pennies and got another nickel. Then Ferdie looked at the two nickels in his hand, and his face grew sad. "I used to have ten pennies and now all I have are these two nickels. I think I'm losing money on this deal."

Is Ferdie losing money? Why not? No, two nickels are worth ten pennies.

How many cents are two nickels worth? ten

Ferdie put the two nickels in the machine and out dropped the Crispy Cracklers. Ferdie opened them and began eating. "What a marvelous cracker!" he said. "Why, it's worth more than two nickels. It's almost worth a dime!"

Does that make sense? Why not? No, two nickels have the same value as a dime.

. . . the end

◆ **STORY 11** **Ferdie Buys a Snack**

Story Problems

1 Manolita had a nickel. She traded it for pennies at Mr. Muddle's store.

How many pennies did she get? five

2 Portia ate half a muffin. Ferdie ate just as much as Portia.

How many muffins did the two of them eat together? one

3 Ferdie is one year older than Portia, his younger sister. "I'll catch up," said Portia.

Will she? Why not? Ferdie will always be one year older.

How old will Portia be when Ferdie is ten? nine

4 "I have three coins in my purse," said Ms. Eng, "and together they make 15 cents."

Can anyone figure out what they are? three nickels

"In my coat pocket I have only two coins," said Ms. Eng, "and together they make 15 cents."

What are they? a dime and a nickel

"That's nothing," said Ferdie. "I have four coins in my pocket, and together they make eight cents. I'll bet nobody can figure out what I have!"

Can you? a nickel and three pennies

5   Mr. Mudancia had a desk with six empty drawers in it. He filled two of the drawers with dirt and is growing mushrooms in them.

What does he have now? a desk with four empty drawers, plus two drawers with mushrooms

6   Loretta the Letter Carrier and her husband, Roger, had two dogs and a cat. Yesterday one of the dogs had three puppies.

How many dogs does she have now? five

7   Loretta and Roger's cat had five kittens. Loretta gave one to Manolita, one to Willy, and one to Marcus. But Marcus's mother wouldn't let him keep his, so he had to give it back.

How many kittens does Loretta have now? three

8   Portia had nine dandelions. She gave away all but two of them.

How many are left? two

9   Mr. Muddle gets lost every time he goes downtown at night. He went downtown six times last week.

How many times did he get lost? can't tell

What do you need to know before you can be sure? how many times he went downtown at night

Ms. Eng's Fish Stories

Ms. Eng likes to go fishing and she likes to tell other people about it, but sometimes she doesn't tell enough. One day when she got back from a fishing trip, the children were all out in front of her house to meet her.

"How many fish did you catch?" they asked.

"Well," said Ms. Eng, "in the morning I caught four fish and in the afternoon I caught some more. So you should be able to figure out how many I caught all together."

Can you figure it out? Why not?
No, she doesn't say how many she caught in the afternoon.

"Wait a minute," said Marcus. "How many fish did you catch in the afternoon?"

"I caught only two fish in the afternoon," said Ms. Eng. "They weren't biting as well then."

Now can you figure out how many fish she caught all together? six

"You caught six fish!" the children all shouted, except for Ferdie. Ferdie thought Ms. Eng had caught only two fish.

What did Ferdie forget about? the fish she caught in the morning

"Did you catch any big fish?" asked Willy.

"Indeed I did!" said Ms. Eng. "I caught one that is almost as big as the biggest fish I ever caught."

"How long is the fish?" Willy asked.

"You should be able to figure that out for yourself," said Ms. Eng, "when I tell you that the big fish I caught today

is only 1 centimeter shorter than the biggest fish I ever caught."

Can you figure it out? no

"I wish I knew the answer," said Willy.

"Wait a minute," said Marcus. "I have a question, Ms. Eng."

What question do you think Marcus is going to ask? How long was the biggest fish she ever caught?

Marcus asked, "How long was the biggest fish you ever caught?"

"It was 41 centimeters long," said Ms. Eng.

Now can you figure out how long the fish is that Ms. Eng caught today? yes, by subtracting one from 41

How much shorter is it than the biggest fish? 1 cm

◆ **STORY 12 Ms. Eng's Fish Stories**

"You caught a fish 40 centimeters long!" cried Portia.

How long is that? Show with your hands. [Demonstrate.]

Is that very long for a fish? for some kinds of fish, but not for the biggest fish a person has ever caught

Ms. Eng took a basket out of her car and showed the children the 40-centimeter-long fish.

"You may think this is a big fish,"

Ms. Eng said, "but it's nothing compared to the one that got away."

"How long was it?" Ferdie asked.

"I don't know how long it was," said Ms. Eng, "but it had eyes as big as my husband's pocket watch."

"Wow!" said Ferdie. "A giant fish!"

"Wait a minute," said Marcus. "I have a question."

What question do you think Marcus will ask? How big is Mr. Eng's pocket watch?

"How big is Mr. Eng's pocket watch?" Marcus asked.

"About a centimeter wide," said Ms. Eng.

How wide is that? Show with your fingers. [Demonstrate.]

"Yes," said Ms. Eng, "my husband has the smallest pocket watch I've ever seen. And the fish didn't have very big eyes, either. But it was heavy. I'll bet that fish weighed twice as much as my Aunt Minnie's hairbrush."

"That's not very heavy," said Manolita. "Everybody knows that a hairbrush doesn't weigh much!"

"Wait a minute," said Marcus. "I have another question."

What question do you think Marcus will ask this time? How much does Aunt Minnie's hairbrush weigh?

"How much does your Aunt Minnie's hairbrush weigh?" Marcus asked.

"It weighs 5 kilograms," said Ms. Eng. "It is a very big hairbrush. My Aunt Minnie uses it to brush her pet giraffe."

Now can you figure out how many kilograms the fish weighed? about ten kilograms

. . . *the end*

◆ **STORY 12 Ms. Eng's Fish Stories**

Story Problems

❶ "I always carry five pens with me," said Ms. Eng, "but I've lost two of them. I'm on my way to buy some more."

How many pens does she have with her now? three

How many pens do you think she will buy? two

❷ Manolita is having a birthday party. She just blew out six candles on the cake. Two candles are still burning.

How old is Manolita? eight

❸ Portia weighed 40 pounds. Over summer vacation she grew 1 inch and gained 0 pounds.

How much does she weigh now? 40 pounds

❹ Ferdie had five tadpoles. Something happened to one of them.

How many tadpoles does he have now? can't tell

What do you need to know? whether that one is no longer a tadpole; [If a child insists that one turned into a frog or died, ask: Do you know for sure? What if it just got bigger? How many would he have then?]

5 "I'll bet my paper airplane can fly farther than yours," said Manolita. Willy threw his plane and it went 4 yards. Manolita threw hers and it went 3 yards. Then she threw it again and it went 3 more yards.

Whose airplane can fly farther? Willy's

6 Marcus is growing fast. He grew 2 inches in just nine months.

How tall is he now? can't tell

What do you need to know before you can figure it out? how tall he was

7 Ferdie's pencil broke near the middle. He wonders if he has more than half or less than half of it left.

How could he find out? by seeing which piece is longer

8 Mrs. Mudancia drove Manolita to her friend Joyce's house and then drove her home. Joyce lives 2 miles away.

How far did Manolita ride all together? 4 miles

9 Willy can wear Ferdie's shoes, but Ferdie can't get into Willy's shoes.

Who has bigger feet? Ferdie

**STORY
13**

**THINKING
STORY**

Manolita's Magnificent Minus Machine

anolita was dreaming about a giant machine again. This machine was just like the ones she had dreamed about before, except that if you put in five things, it would give back four; if you put in six things, it would give back five; if you put in nine things, it would give back eight.

What was the machine doing?
subtracting 1

When Manolita woke up, she decided that she could build a machine like that. She found a big, big box. On it she painted a sign that said "MAGNIFICENT MINUS MACHINE. Whatever you put in to the top, you get back one fewer at the bottom. FREE!"

Manolita put the machine out by the sidewalk and hid inside it. Soon children began flocking around the machine and reading the sign. "It's free!" Portia said.

Marcus was the first to try it. He put in seven sticks. The machine went "Glinka-Glinka" and out came six sticks at the bottom.

What do you think made the machine go "Glinka-Glinka"? Manolita

What do you think happened to the other stick that Marcus put into the machine? Manolita kept it.

Ferdie wanted to try the machine next. He put in nine marbles.

How many marbles will he get back?
eight

"Hey," said Ferdie, "the machine kept one of my marbles!" Ferdie was angry and walked away.

Marcus tried the machine again. He put in four crayons.

How many crayons will he get back?
three

The machine went "Glinka-Glinka" and out came three crayons at the bottom. Marcus didn't like that very much, but he said, "I'm going to put them back into the machine, and maybe this time more will come out." He put his three crayons into the machine.

Will he get back more than three?
no

This time the machine gave him back only two crayons. That made Marcus angry, and he walked away.

Portia felt in her pocket and found five pumpkin seeds that she had been saving to plant. She dropped them into the Magnificent Minus Machine and waited eagerly to see what would happen.

What will happen? She will get back four seeds.

◆ STORY 13 Manolita's Magnificent Minus Machine

The machine went "Glinka-Glinka," and out came four pumpkin seeds. "Nasty machine!" said Portia, and she walked away. Soon none of the children would have anything to do with Manolita's Magnificent Minus Machine.

Why not? It kept subtracting one.

Then Willy the Wisher came along. He had just finished eating a banana. "I wish I had someplace to put this banana peel," said Willy. "I wish there were a wastebasket right here." Then he noticed the Magnificent Minus Machine. He put the banana peel into the top.

What do you think will come out the bottom? nothing

When you put in one banana peel, how many banana peels do you get back? zero

The machine went "Glinka-Glinka," but no banana peel came out at the bottom. After that, whenever people had some trash to get rid of, they put it into Manolita's Magnificent Minus Machine.

. . . the end

◆ STORY 13   Manolita's Magnificent Minus Machine

Story Problems

❶ Manolita dreamed about a different kind of machine.
She put in three acorns and got back six. She put in
two cards and got back four. She put in one card and
got back two.

What was the machine doing? doubling the number

**What will Manolita get back if she puts in four
sticks?** eight sticks

❷ All the children were eating pizza. Willy was
the second one to finish. Manolita was the fourth.

Who ate faster—Manolita or Willy? Willy

How can you tell? He finished before Manolita.

❸ Portia saves two pennies every day.

How long will it take her to save ten cents? five days

Ferdie saves one penny a day.

How long will it take him to save ten cents? ten days

❹ Portia was learning to walk on stilts. The first day
she could take two steps before falling. The next day
she could take four steps. The next day she could
take six steps.

**How many steps would you guess she could take
the day after that? Why do you think so?**
[Any answer will do, although eight is the obvious one.
What is of interest is the reason given.]

5 Willy got four strawberries. "I'm only going to eat two strawberries every day," said Willy, "so they'll last a long time."

How many days will they last? two

6 Portia walked one block by herself. Then she walked three times as far with her friend Taro.

How many blocks did Portia walk all together? four

7 Willy walked half a block to the library. Then he walked half a block to get home.

How many blocks did he walk all together? one

8 Ferdie decided he was going to be nice to five people today. He tried and tried, but so far he has managed to be nice to only two people—himself and Mr. Muddle.

How many more people does Ferdie need to be nice to? three

9 "This is the fourth time I've been to the zoo," said Portia.

How many times had she been to the zoo before? three

10 Portia had four dolls. She gave a doll to Willy and a tennis ball to Manolita.

How many dolls does Portia have left? three

STORY
14

THINKING STORY

Mr. Mudancia Makes Lunch

One day it was Mr. Mudancia's turn to make lunch. But, of course, he wasn't happy making an ordinary lunch. Mr. Mudancia decided to change everything for lunch—just a little.

The first thing Mr. Mudancia did was take out three stalks of celery and put them on a plate. But that didn't look like very much, so he changed the celery a little. He cut each stalk of celery in half.

How many pieces of celery are there now? six

Is there more celery than before? no, just smaller pieces

Next Mr. Mudancia took out six muffins "These look like tasty muffins," said Mr. Mudancia, "but they're on the small side. I think I'll change them a little."

He took two muffins, put one on top of the other, and squeezed them until they were mashed together.

What did he make? one big, messy muffin

Then he did the same thing with two other muffins, and then with two other muffins after that.

Now how many muffins does Mr. Mudancia have all together?
three

"Three big muffins," said Mr. Mudancia. "That's just right: one for me, one for my dear wife, and one for my little Manolita."

Next Mr. Mudancia took two pitchers of juice out of the refrigerator. There were 3 cups of grape juice and 2 cups of tomato juice. He mixed them together.

How many cups of juice does he have now? 5

What do you think it tastes like?
not very good

◆ **STORY 14 Mr. Mudancia Makes Lunch**

Finally Mr. Mudancia took out some vegetables. There were green peas and chickpeas all mixed together in a bowl. He measured them with a big spoon. There were ten spoonfuls. "We have ten tasty spoonfuls of vegetables," said Mr. Mudancia, "but I think I'll change them a little."

He carefully picked out all the green peas. When he was done, there were six spoonfuls of chickpeas left.

Can you figure out how many spoonfuls of green peas he took out? four

At lunchtime Manolita was amazed. "These muffins are much bigger than they used to be," Manolita said. "What did you do to them, Papa?"

"Just used a little squeeze-power," said Mr. Mudancia.

Then Manolita tasted the juice. She took a sip, made a face, and put it down. "I don't know what you did to this juice," said Manolita, "but I wish you could do something to change it back to the way it was!"

Could Mr. Mudancia change the juice back to the way it was? Why not?
No, the juice is already mixed together.

. . . *the end*

◆ **STORY 14 Mr. Mudancia Makes Lunch**

Story Problems

❶ Mr. Muddle said, "I started out with three tickets to the circus, and then either I gave one away or somebody gave me one—I can't remember which."

How many tickets does Mr. Muddle have now? two or four; you can't tell for sure

What do you need to know to be sure? whether he gave one ticket away or someone gave him one

❷ When his father came into the house, Willy was standing in the middle of the stairs. Willy went up two steps. Then he went down three steps and stayed there.

Is Willy higher or lower now than when his father came in? lower

How much lower? one step

❸ Mr. Muddle has three lamps in his living room. Each lamp has a lightbulb in it, but two of the bulbs have been burned out for a long time, so in the evening he always sits by the third lamp. Last night the bulb in that lamp burned out, too, so Mr. Muddle had to go to bed. This morning he went to the hardware store and bought four lightbulbs.

Will Mr. Muddle have enough bulbs for all the lamps in his living room? yes, and one extra

4 Ms. Eng bought two skirts and a sweater for her daughter Patty. Then she bought exactly the same things for her other daughter, Pitty.

How many skirts did she buy all together? four

How many sweaters did she buy all together? two

5 Mr. Mudancia had a belt with eight holes in it, but he changed it a little. He filled in half of the holes.

How many holes are left in the belt? four

6 Portia has an extra wheel fastened to the back of her wagon in case she has wheel trouble.

How many wheels are on the wagon? five

7 Ping used to walk a block to school. Now she has to walk twice as far.

How far does she have to walk now? two blocks

8 Chewies cost ten cents apiece. Ferdie bought one of them with money from his piggy bank. Marcus bought three of them with money his father gave him.

How much did Ferdie pay? 10¢

9 "I'll give you ten cents, Marcus, if you mail this letter for me," said Mr. Breezy, "and I'll give you twice as much if you go very fast." Marcus ran like an antelope (that's very fast).

How much money did Marcus earn? 20¢

How Ms. Eng Doubled Her Money

"**Y**ou have two of everything, Ms. Eng," said Marcus. "You must be rich."

"That's right," said Ms. Eng.

"How did you get that way?"

"Simple," said Ms. Eng. "By getting lots of money."

"But how did you do that?" Portia asked.

"I'll tell you how it all started," said Ms. Eng. "One day when I was a young girl I found a quarter on the sidewalk. I used it to buy something. "

"What?" Ferdie asked.

"A handkerchief, of course."

"Did you have a cold?"

"No," said Ms. Eng, "but I soon met a woman who did, and she gave me some money for the handkerchief. That's how I started to get rich."

"Wait a minute," said Marcus. "I have a question."

What question do you think Marcus will ask? How much did the handkerchief sell for?

"My question," said Marcus, "is how much did you sell the handkerchief for?"

"Twice as much as I paid for it," said Ms. Eng.

How much did Ms. Eng pay for the handkerchief? one quarter

So how many quarters did she get for the handkerchief? two

How much money is two quarters? 50¢

"You got a dollar!" Portia piped up.

"That's not so much," said Ferdie. "I had a dollar once."

"Ah," said Ms. Eng, "but I used my dollar to buy a sick canary."

"Why did you buy a sick one?" Portia asked.

"So that when it got well and started to sing I could sell it for more money. So I sold it for more than I paid for it, and . . ."

"Wait a minute," said Marcus.

What is Marcus going to ask? How much did the canary sell for?

"How much did you sell the canary for?" Marcus asked.

"For a dollar more than I paid for it," Ms. Eng answered.

How much money did she have after she sold the canary? $2

"So you had 50 cents," said Marcus.

"Yes," said Ms. Eng. "And with the 50 cents I bought some pencils. Then I sold the pencils to my friends, you see, and made more money. Can you figure out how much I made?"

"A nickel?" Ferdie guessed.

"Wait a minute," said Marcus.

What questions does Marcus need to ask? How many pencils did she have, and how much did she sell them for?

"How many pencils did you have, and how much did you sell them for?" Marcus asked.

"I had ten pencils," said Ms. Eng, "and I sold them for ten cents apiece."

Can you figure out how much money she got all together from selling the pencils? $1

Try counting by tens.

◆ STORY 15 How Ms. Eng Doubled Her Money

"You had two dollars!" the children said.

"Right," said Ms. Eng. "And I used the two dollars to buy a shoe."

"One shoe?" asked Ferdie.

"That's right."

"But one shoe isn't worth anything," Ferdie said.

"This one was," said Ms. Eng, "because I knew a man who had one shoe just like it for the other foot. So he was glad to pay me what I asked for the shoe, and with that money . . ."

"Wait a minute," said Marcus.

What question is Marcus going to ask? How much money did the man pay for the shoe?

"How much money did you ask the man to pay for the shoe?" Marcus asked.

"Why, I asked him to pay twice as much as I paid," said Ms. Eng. "I always like to double my money."

How much did Ms. Eng pay for the shoe? $2

What's twice as much? So how much money did she get for the shoe? $4

"Four dollars!" said Ferdie. "You really were getting rich!"

"But I didn't stop there," said Ms. Eng. "I used the four dollars to buy a clock with no hands."

"What good is a clock with no hands?" Portia asked.

"I don't know," said Ms. Eng. "In fact, I never could find anyone who wanted to buy the clock, so I still have it. If you happen to know anyone who wants a clock with no hands, I'll sell it for a good price."

"What price?" asked Marcus.

"Why, only twice as much as I paid for it," said Ms. Eng.

How much did she pay for the clock? $4

How much does she want to sell it for? $8

"But wait," said Manolita, who had been quiet until then. "You were going to tell us how you got rich. If you bought the clock for four dollars and you still have the clock, then you couldn't get rich that way."

Why not? How much money did Ms. Eng have left after she bought the clock with no hands? none

"Oh, I forgot to tell you one little thing," said Ms. Eng. "When I opened up that old clock with no hands, I found it had half a million dollars inside."

. . . the end

◆ **STORY 15** How Ms. Eng Doubled Her Money

Story Problems

❶ If Mr. Breezy works all day, he can wash half the windows in his house.

How many days will it take him to wash all the windows? two

❷ Marcus had eight shells that he found on the beach. He showed two of them to his friend Willy.

How many shells did Marcus have then? eight

❸ "What a smart baby!" said Portia. "He spoke his first word when he was only ten months old, and he spoke his second word when he was only nine months old."

What's wrong with what Portia said? He spoke the second word before the first.

❹ A friendly baker gave a group of children two Danish rolls. "Break each one in half," he said.

How many pieces did the children have after they broke the rolls? four

There were eight children.

Did each of them get half a roll? no

What could they do? break each of the four pieces in half

❺ Ferdie had eight marbles and Marcus had four. Mr. Breezy gave two marbles to the boy who had fewer.

How many marbles does Ferdie have now? eight

❻ The Mudancias used to be able to bake enchiladas in 15 minutes, but Mr. Mudancia changed the oven a little. Now it takes ten minutes longer.

How many minutes does it take to bake enchiladas now? 25

7 Once Mr. Eng grew a beard. It was 10 inches long, but Mr. Mudancia changed it a little. He cut off 8 inches.

How long was Mr. Eng's beard after Mr. Mudancia changed it? 2 inches

How long is that? Show with your fingers. [Demonstrate.]

8 Mr. Mudancia had a necktie that was 44 inches long. He cut an inch off one end and an inch off the other end.

How long is the piece of necktie now? 42 inches

9 There is a snail in Willy's fishbowl that is trying to crawl up the side. Every day it climbs up 3 inches and every night it slides down 3 inches.

How far up will the snail get after four days and four nights? 0 inches

10 There is another snail in Willy's fishbowl that does a little better. Every day it climbs up 3 inches, but at night it slides down only 1 inch.

How far up will the snail get after four days and four nights? 8 inches [Suggest that the children use a ruler or number line to work it out.]

11 Mr. Mudancia used to be able to seat five people around his dinner table. He made the table bigger, and now he can fit three more people.

How many people can sit around the dinner table now? eight

12 Manolita had seven colored markers. She sold some of them to Portia for 25¢ each.

How many colored markers does Manolita have left? can't tell

What do you need to know before you can tell? how many she sold

STORY
16

THINKING STORY

The Third House on Fungo Street

One day Ferdie and Portia were walking along with their friend Loretta as she was delivering the mail. "Here's a hard one to figure out," said Loretta, looking at an envelope. "This is a letter for someone named Sandy Bright, and the only address on it is 'Third House on Fungo Street.'"

"That should be easy," said Ferdie. "Fungo Street is so short there aren't very many houses on it."

"Then perhaps you can tell me which house it is," said Loretta the Letter Carrier, as they started walking along Fungo Street.

There are just 13 houses on Fungo Street, and this map shows where they are. The numbers are house numbers.

[Show the illustration.]
"I know which house it is," said Ferdie. He counted off "One, two, three" and pointed to house number 1. "That's the third house on Fungo Street," he said. Ferdie marched up to the door of house number 6 and called, "We have a letter here for Sandy Bright!"

"Nobody named Sandy Bright lives here," said a gruff man who came to the door.

What could be wrong? What other house could be the third house on Fungo Street? number 5

"I know," said Ferdie. "It must be house number 5, across the street. That's the third house on Fungo Street too, only on the other side of the street!"

◆ STORY 16   The Third House on Fungo Street

They went across to house number 5, but no Sandy Bright lived there either. "I give up," said Ferdie. "Whoever wrote that letter didn't know where Sandy Bright lives."

Then Portia said, "I have an idea where the third house on Fungo Street might be."

Do you have an idea where it could be? It could be the third house from the other end.

"Maybe it's the third house from the *other* end," said Portia.

"We'll try your idea," said Loretta.

Which house is the third house from the other end? number 9

Which other house is also the third one from the other end? number 8

They started at the other end and counted house number 13, house number 11, and house number 9. "This must be it," said Ferdie. "House number 9 is the third house on Fungo Street."

So they knocked on the door. Mr. Muddle came to the door and said hello. Loretta the Letter Carrier said, "You don't have anyone named Sandy Bright living in your house, do you, Mr. Muddle?"

"Not that I can think of," said Mr. Muddle.

"There's only one other house it could be," said Portia.

What house is that? number 8

They went up to house number 8. A big man with reddish-brown hair was sitting on the front porch. "Is there anyone here named Sandy Bright?" asked Loretta the Letter Carrier.

"I'm Sandy Bright," said the man. "I wondered what you were doing, walking up and down the street that way."

They gave him the letter and walked away. "I'm afraid I have another hard letter to figure out," said Loretta. "This one is addressed to just 'Otto, The Fifth House on Fungo Street.'"

Which houses could be the fifth house on Fungo Street? Can you find four different ones? numbers 5, 4, 10, 9

First they tried house number 5, but no one named Otto lived there. Then they tried house number 4. No Otto. Then they started counting from the other end and tried house number 10. Still no Otto.

Which house haven't they tried yet? number 9

Who lives there? Mr. Muddle

It must be house number 9," said Portia. "But that's Mr. Muddle's house."

"Hey," said Ferdie, "something's wrong here. Mr. Muddle's house was the third house on Fungo Street. How can it be the fifth house on Fungo Street too?"

Can you figure out how it can be the third house and the fifth house at the same time? It depends on which end of the street you're starting from.

Ferdie thought for a minute and then said, "I get it. Mr. Muddle's house is the third house from one end and it's the fifth house from the other end."

They went up to Mr. Muddle's house again and knocked on the door. "Hello again, Mr. Muddle," said Loretta. "This time we're looking for somebody named Otto, who lives in the fifth house on Fungo Street."

Mr. Muddle was delighted. "That's me," he said, "Otto Muddle. Ah, I see you have my letter. I wrote it myself."

Portia asked, "Why did you write yourself a letter, Mr. Muddle?"

"I can't remember," said Mr. Muddle. "I'll have to read it and find out. Maybe it contains important news."

"If you write an answer to that letter," said Loretta, "I hope you'll put your whole name and your house number on it. Otherwise you may never get it."

"That would be dreadful," said Mr. Muddle. "Then I'd never know what happened, would I?"

. . . the end

◆ **STORY 16 The Third House on Fungo Street**

Story Problems

1 Ferdie sat in the first chair. Portia sat in the fourth chair.

How many chairs are between them? two

Which chairs are they? second and third

2 Mr. Muddle decided to give a prize to the third person who came into his store that day. First came Marcus, then came Manolita, then Loretta the Letter Carrier brought in some mail; then came Portia; and then came Ferdie.

Who got the prize? Loretta

The next time Mr. Muddle decided to give the prize to the fourth *child* who came in. First came Ferdie, then Marcus, then Portia, then Loretta the Letter Carrier, then Ms. Eng, then Willy, then Manolita, then Ferdie again.

Who got the prize this time? Willy

3 Mr. Muddle drinks half a container of milk a day. He opened a container of milk just this morning.

When will he have to open another container? in two days, or the day after tomorrow

4 "I'm trying to save up ten cereal box tops to get a free kite," said Marcus. "I've already saved two."

How many more box tops does he need? eight

5 Ferdie had 15 cents. His mother gave him a quarter to go buy a newspaper for her.

How much money will Ferdie have after he buys the newspaper? 15¢, if the newspaper costs 25¢

6 "How many years have you owned this store?" somebody asked Mr. Muddle. "I don't remember," said Mr. Muddle, "but I do know I was 40 years old when I got it, and now I'm 45 years old."

Can you figure out how long he's had the store? five years

7 Manolita's house is a block away from Portia and Ferdie's. Yesterday Manolita walked over to Portia and Ferdie's to play. When it was time for dinner, Manolita walked home. Then she walked back to Portia and Ferdie's house to spend the night.

How far did Manolita walk all together? three blocks

8 All the children are sitting in a row at the movie. Listen and figure out who is sitting next to Willy: Willy is sitting in the third seat. Ferdie is in the first seat, Marcus is in the fourth seat, Manolita is in the fifth seat, and Portia is in the second seat.

Who is sitting next to Willy? Portia and Marcus

9 Manolita found half a bagel in the cookie jar, half a bagel in the refrigerator, and half a bagel in a paper bag.

If she put them all together, how many bagels would she have? three halves or $1\frac{1}{2}$

10 Marcus invited two boys for lunch. Each of the boys took his little brother along too.

How many boys went to Marcus's house for lunch? four

11 Mr. Mudancia had a candle that was 10 inches long. He let it burn until only 8 inches were left, and then he cut an inch off the bottom.

How long is the candle now? 7 inches

12 Six children had a race down to the beach. Manolita was the fourth child to get there.

How many children got there after she did? two

STORY
17

THINKING STORY

The Lemonade War

One day when Ferdie was walking along the sidewalk he saw Marcus standing behind a box. On the box were a pitcher and some glasses and a sign that said "Lemonade 5¢."

"What are you doing?" Ferdie asked.

"Selling lemonade," said Marcus.

"Do you get to keep the money?"

"Yes," said Marcus, "and I've already sold two glasses of lemonade."

How much money has Marcus made?
10¢

"That's a great idea," said Ferdie. "I think I'll do it too." So he got some lemonade and glasses and a box from his mother and set up a lemonade stand on the sidewalk, right next to Marcus's. But Ferdie was a little greedy. He wanted to make more money than Marcus, so he wrote on his sign "Lemonade 6¢."

Two children, Janet and Ken, came along. They read both signs and then they bought some lemonade from Marcus.

Why do you think they did that?
Marcus's lemonade was cheaper.

"Hey!" said Ferdie. "Why didn't you buy from me?"

"You charge too much," Ken said. "Why should we pay you six cents when Marcus sells it for five cents?"

Ferdie thought about it and then he had an idea. He changed the sign so that now it said "Lemonade 4¢."

Why did he do that? so that people will buy his lemonade instead of Marcus's

Soon Manolita came along. She read both signs and went to Ferdie's stand. She held up a nickel and said, "One glass of lemonade, please."

How much is a nickel worth? 5¢

"My lemonade is four cents," said Ferdie. "Don't you have four cents?"

"No."

"Too bad," he said. "Come back when you do."

Instead, Manolita went to Marcus's stand and bought lemonade from him for a nickel.

What should Ferdie have done? given change

How much money should he have given Manolita? 1¢

"You should have taken the nickel," said Marcus, "and given Manolita a penny change."

"Oh," said Ferdie, "thanks. I'll remember to do that next time."

The next person to come along, Mr. Burns, had a dime. He handed it to Ferdie and asked for a glass of lemonade. Ferdie poured him a glass, took the dime, and gave him back one penny.

Was that right? How much should Ferdie have given him? 6¢

Why do you suppose Ferdie gave him just a penny? That's what he should have given Manolita.

◆ STORY 17 The Lemonade War

Mr. Burns was angry. "That's not enough change," he said. "Here, keep your lemonade and give me back my dime." Then he took his dime to Marcus's stand and bought a glass of lemonade with it. Marcus gave him the right change.

How much change did Marcus give him?
5¢

"Next time I'll give the right change," said Ferdie.

Along came Mrs. Downey and Mrs. Kamato. They went to Ferdie's stand and each one asked for a glass of lemonade. Ferdie was delighted. "You came to the right place, ladies. Best lemonade. Best prices. And I always give the right change."

Mrs. Downey gave Ferdie a dime. Ferdie carefully counted out six cents change for her.

Why did he give her six cents? He thought she was paying for one glass of lemonade.

"Oh," said Mrs. Downey, "but I wanted to pay for *both* glasses of lemonade with my dime."

"Excuse me," said Ferdie, and he gave her six more cents change.

Was that the right thing to do? no

How much change did Ferdie give Mrs. Downey all together? 12¢

How can you tell that's too much? How much money did she give him? 10¢

Should you ever get more change than the amount you paid? no

When Mrs. Downey and Mrs. Kamato left, Ferdie said, "At last I've sold some lemonade. I'm rich! I'm rich! I'm rich!" Then he counted out his money and found that he had less than when he started.

Why did he have less? He gave too much change.

"I've been robbed!" Ferdie screamed.

"No, you haven't," said a voice. It was Mrs. Downey, who had come back. "I just wanted to see if you would figure out that you made a mistake," she said. She gave Ferdie ten cents and told him to be more careful with his money next time.

"There isn't going to be a next time," said Ferdie. "I'm getting out of this business while I still have some money left."

Ferdie picked up his lemonade and glasses and box and sign, and left. As he was walking away he heard Marcus shouting, "Get your lemonade here, folks! Only six cents!"

What had Marcus done? raised his price

Why could Marcus charge six cents now? no competition

. . . the end

◆ STORY 17 The Lemonade War

Story Problems

1 "Look at the nickel I found," said Willy.

"I could use a nickel like that," said his friend Ferdie.

"I'll give you four cents for it."

Should Willy sell it to him? Why not? No, a nickel is five cents, not four cents.

2 Marcus brushes his teeth four minutes almost every day, but yesterday he was lazy and brushed them only half that long.

How many minutes did he brush his teeth yesterday? two

3 Manolita bought a toy airplane for two dollars and sold it for one dollar.

How much money did she make? none

How much did she lose? $1

4 Marcus and Manolita were going fishing with Ms. Eng, but first they all had to dig worms. Ms. Eng dug three worms, Marcus dug one, and Manolita dug two.

How many worms did the children dig all together? three

5 One week Portia ate a peanut butter sandwich on Monday and another one on Tuesday. The next week she did the same thing.

How many did she eat in two weeks? four

6 Mr. Muddle is filling a barrel with water. He has already put in 10 gallons.

How many more gallons of water does he have to put in to fill up the barrel all the way? can't tell

What do you need to know? how many gallons the barrel holds

7 "Be sure to bring back the change," said Portia's mother. Portia went to the checkout counter and bought a pack of gum. She gave the grocer five dimes and got back one penny.
How much did the gum cost? 49¢

8 Mr. Mudancia had a 12-string guitar, but he changed it a little. He put four more strings on it.
What kind of guitar does he have now? a 16-string guitar
How many strings does it have now? sixteen

9 Manolita had four crackers. She broke them all in two and ate them.
How many crackers does she have left? zero

10 Mr. Breezy is painting a shed. It has four sides. He can paint two sides in one hour.
How many hours will it take him to paint all four sides? two

11 Every time Portia dips her paintbrush, she can paint one side of a board. She wants to paint three boards on both sides.
How many times will she have to dip her brush? six

12 Willy was able to stand on one foot for eight minutes. "I'll bet I can stand on one foot for nine minutes," said Ferdie. If Ferdie can last three more minutes, he will make it.
How many minutes has Ferdie been standing on one foot so far? six

13 Ferdie and Manolita were arguing about whose jacket pocket was bigger. Ferdie put 15 acorns into his pocket. Manolita put 14 acorns into her pocket, and two of them fell out.
Whose pocket is bigger? Ferdie's
How do you know? He was able to put 15 acorns into his pocket without any falling out.

STORY
18

THINKING
STORY

Mr. Mudancia Changes Houses

One day Mr. Mudancia made the mistake of changing his house into a bowling alley, and then his family had no place to live. "You can stay in our summer house," said Ms. Eng, who had two of everything, even houses. "Just make yourselves at home there and change anything into the way you want."

The Mudancias were very pleased with the Engs' summer house, but as soon as they moved in Mr. Mudancia started to change things a little. There was a clock on the wall that looked like this.

[Show the illustration.]

How many points does the clock have? eight

Mr. Mudancia changed the clock a little by taking off all the long points.

How many points are left? four

"I hope the Engs like a four-pointed clock," said Manolita.

There was a poster on the wall that looked like this:

[Cover the illustration on the right and show the one on the left.]
How many corners does the poster have? Count them. four

Mr. Mudancia cut off one of the corners so that the poster looked like this.
[Show the second illustration.]
How many corners does the poster have now? Count them. five

Mr. Mudancia liked the way the poster looked so much that he clipped off the other three corners the same way.

How many corners does the poster have now? Picture it in your mind. eight

"I hope the Engs like an eight-cornered poster," said Mrs. Mudancia.

On the floor of the summer house was a very thick rug. It was 1 inch thick.

How thick is that? Show with your fingers. [Demonstrate.]

◆ STORY 18 Mr. Mudancia Changes Houses

Mr. Mudancia changed the rug a little. He cut it in half and put one half on top of the other.

How thick is it now? 2 inches

"I'm sure the Engs will be happy to have a rug 2 inches thick on the floor," said Mr. Mudancia.

"I'm not so sure," said Mrs. Mudancia. "The rug is twice as thick as it was before, but it isn't as long."

How long is it now? half as long

There was a fishbowl in the summer house. Mr. Mudancia changed the bowl by cutting it in half from top to bottom. **How many fishbowls do the Mudancias have now?** none

They don't have any fishbowl, because neither half holds water. So they put the fish in the bathtub. Now they have no fishbowl and no place to take a bath, either.

. . . the end

◆ **STORY 18   Mr. Mudancia Changes Houses**

Story Problems

1 Do you know how a paper clip is shaped?
[Show the illustration or, if you're working with a large
group, draw a paper clip on the chalkboard.]

Mrs. Mudancia had a paper clip that was 2 inches long.
She straightened it so there was no more bend.

How long is the straightened paper clip? about 5 inches;
depends on the size of the paper clip

2 Mr. Mudancia had a woolen scarf 40 inches long. He cut
10 inches off one end and sewed it onto the other end.

How long is the scarf now? 40 inches

3 Mr. Mudancia had a hose that was 6 yards long. He made
it a yard shorter at one end, and then he made it 2 yards
longer at the other end.

How long is the hose now? 7 yards

4 Mr. Muddle lives a block and a half from his store.
He walks to the store in the morning and walks home
in the afternoon.

How far does he walk all together? three blocks

5 Willy has ten marbles. Seven of them are little.

How many of them are round? all ten

6 Ferdie and Manolita wanted to buy some popcorn
together, but it cost 50 cents. "I'll pay a quarter and
you pay the rest," said Ferdie.

Is that fair? yes

How much would Manolita have to pay? 25¢

7 There are four doors in Mr. Mudancia's house, and each one had a doorknob. But Mr. Mudancia changed that. He put an extra doorknob on each door.

How many doorknobs are there now? eight

8 Ferdie was carrying three jars of pickles at the store, but he dropped two of them.

How many good bottles are left? can't tell

What do you need to know? how many broke

9 Portia lives on the second floor.

How many floors down does she have to go to get to the basement? two

10 Mr. Tomkins drives a city bus. One day four people got on at his first stop. At the next stop one person got off. At the next stop two people got on.

How many passengers were on the bus then? five

11 Manolita belongs to a scout troop. There were ten scouts the first year. The next year five scouts moved away, but there was one new scout.

How many scouts were in the troop then? six

12 Mr. Eng used to weigh 10 pounds more than Mr. Muddle, but now Mr. Muddle weighs 15 pounds less than Mr. Eng.

This one is tricky. [Read it again.]

What could have happened? What else?
Mr. Eng gained weight, or Mr. Muddle lost weight.

STORY
19

THINKING
STORY

Trouble in the Garden

In the springtime Ferdie went out to the country to help his grandfather plant his garden. The first thing that Grandpa wanted Ferdie to do was dig holes to plant some little trees in. "Please dig the holes exactly 8 inches deep," said Grandpa.

Ferdie grabbed a shovel and dug the holes in a hurry. "I'm done, Grandpa!" said Ferdie. "What's next?"

"We'll see," said Grandpa. He took a ruler and measured the holes. They were all 10 inches deep.

Is that what they should have been? no

Were they too deep or not deep enough? too deep

"Rats," said Ferdie, "I made the holes too deep. Now I'll have to start over and dig new ones."

"I think there might be an easier way," said Grandpa.

Can you think of an easier way? put some dirt into the holes

How much dirt should Ferdie put into the holes to make them right? enough to fill 2 inches

Grandpa showed Ferdie how to pack 2 inches of dirt into the holes so they would be just 8 inches deep. Then he gave Ferdie some onions to plant. "Please plant them 5 inches apart," said Grandpa.

Ferdie took the onions and quickly planted a row of them. "I'm done," he said. "What's next?"

"Take your time," said Grandpa. He took his ruler and measured how far apart the onions were. "These onions are 10 inches apart," said Grandpa. "I asked you to plant them 5 inches apart."

How far apart is 10 inches? Show with your hands. [Demonstrate.]

How far apart is 5 inches? Show with your hands. [Demonstrate.]

"Rats," said Ferdie. "I'll have to pull out the onions and start all over."

Does he really have to pull them out and start over? no

What else could he do? He could plant another onion between every two that he had planted.

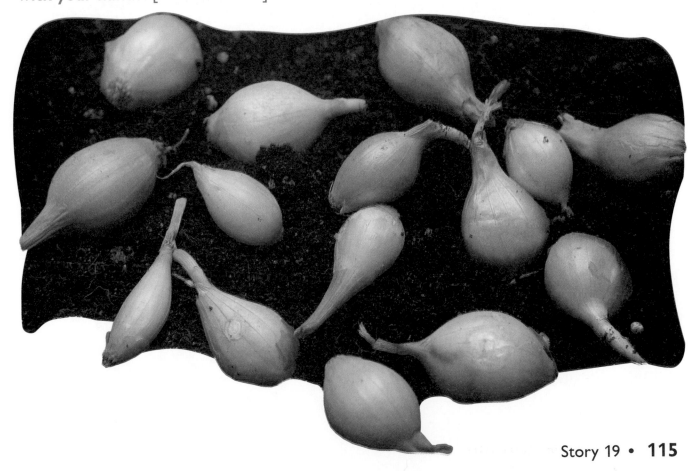

◆ STORY 19 Trouble in the Garden

Grandpa showed Ferdie how he could stick another onion between every two onions that he had planted. Then the onions would all be 5 inches apart.

For his next job Grandpa gave Ferdie a package of radish seeds. "Please spread this out so that the whole package makes one row," said Grandpa.

Ferdie tried to be careful this time. He spread out the radish seeds slowly with his fingers. But when he finished the row he still had half the package left. "I did it wrong," Ferdie moaned. "I was supposed to use up the whole package and I used up only half of it. Now what do I do?"

Can you think of any way he can make it turn out right? He could plant the other half over the same row.

"No problem," said Grandpa. "Just go over the row again and plant the other half of the seeds."

"Now for your last job today," said Grandpa, "I'd like you to plant four rows of beans—exactly four. I have to go back to the house, so I hope you can do this job all right by yourself."

"Don't worry," said Ferdie.

Do you think Ferdie will do it right? no

Keep track of what Ferdie does so you can tell.

Ferdie planted one row of beans, then another row and another row. "Oh, my!" said Ferdie. "I can't remember how many rows I've planted.

Do you know? How many? three

Ferdie didn't remember that he had planted three rows. "I just can't remember," said Ferdie. "I guess I'll have to start over."

Is there any way Ferdie could find out how many he'd planted? by going back and counting

But Ferdie didn't go back and count how many rows he'd planted. Instead, he went ahead and planted four *more* rows of beans. When Grandpa came back from the house, he said, "That looks like a lot of bean rows."

How many rows did Ferdie plant all together? seven

"I lost count," said Ferdie. "I planted some rows, and then I had to start over and plant four more."

"Well," said Grandpa, "it looks as if we're going to have seven rows of beans instead of four. I hope you like beans, Ferdie, because you're going to be eating a lot of them!"

. . . *the end*

◆ **STORY 19   Trouble in the Garden**

Story Problems

1 Ferdie is trying to help by pulling weeds in his grandpa's garden. Every time he pulls up three weeds, he pulls up a bean plant by mistake. Ferdie has pulled up 12 weeds.

Can you figure out how many bean plants he has pulled up? four

2 "That's a tall pear tree, Grandpa," said Ferdie.

"I know it is," said Grandpa. "I climbed up 6 yards in it and then I could just reach the top with a 2-yard pole."

Can you figure out how tall the pear tree is? Not exactly, but it's more than 8 yards.

3 Mr. Mudancia had a picture that was 20 inches high and 30 inches wide. He cut an inch off one side of the picture and an inch off the other side. Then he cut an inch off the top and an inch off the bottom.

What size is the picture now? How high? How wide? 18 inches high, 28 inches wide

4 "When will I ever get done planting these beans?" asked Ferdie. "It took me an hour to plant the first two rows and an hour to plant the next two."

He has four rows left to plant. How many more hours will it take him? two hours, at the rate he is going

5 The Engs live two blocks from the post office. The Breezys live one block farther away from the post office than the Engs do.

Can you tell how far the Engs live from the Breezys? no

What are some possible answers? one block, five blocks

6 Mr. Mudancia had a square handkerchief. He cut the handkerchief in half, going from one corner to another corner.

How many pieces of handkerchief does he have now? two

What shape are they? triangles

7 The Mudancia's bathtub used to be 20 inches deep, but Mr. Mudancia filled in the bottom of it with cement 4 inches deep.

How deep is the tub now? 16 inches

8 Mr. Eng bought a banana for 18¢. He got 2¢ back in change.

How much money had Mr. Eng given the grocer? 20¢

9 Portia has a stack of books that is 8 inches high. Her friend Marcus has a stack of books that is 11 inches high.

Whose stack of books is shorter? Portia's

How much shorter? 3 inches

10 Willy was growing a flower and a weed in his flowerpot. Last week they were both 10 inches high. This week the weed is 14 inches high and the flower is 8 inches high.

What could have happened? the weed grew; something made the flower shorter—the stem broke or the bloom was picked

11 Ferdie, Portia, Marcus, and Willy were drawing pictures. Portia was the second one to finish, Ferdie was the third one to finish, and Marcus was the fourth one to finish.

What can you figure out about Willy? He was first.

STORY
20

THINKING
STORY

How Deep Is the Water?

Mr. Muddle did not go fishing very often, because there were too many things to remember, and he was always forgetting something. But Ferdie had been begging Mr. Muddle to take him fishing for a long time. So one day they packed up Mr. Muddle's boat with everything they thought they would need. They remembered to take fishing poles and string and worms.

Did they forget anything? yes, hooks

Once they got into the boat, they rowed out onto the lake to a place where Mr. Muddle said there were sure to be some fish. But when they were

ready to start fishing, they discovered that they had no fishhooks.

"I did it again," said Mr. Muddle. "I'm sorry. I'm afraid this fishing trip won't be much fun for you."

"That's all right," said Ferdie. "I like just being out here on the lake. I wonder if the water is too deep to stand in."

How could Ferdie find out? by testing the depth of the water with his fishing pole

Ferdie looked around the boat for something he could use to test the depth of the water. "My fishing pole!" Ferdie exclaimed. "This pole is longer than my height," Ferdie said. "Is it longer than your height?" he asked Mr. Muddle.

Mr. Muddle looked carefully at the pole. "It looks like it's exactly as long as my height," said Mr. Muddle.

"Good," said Ferdie. Then he pushed the pole straight down into the water until it touched bottom. There were still 10 inches of the pole sticking out of the water.

Is the water too deep for Mr. Muddle to stand in? no

"The water isn't too deep for the fishing pole, so it isn't too deep for me!" said Mr. Muddle. And he jumped into the water and stood on the bottom.

How much of Mr. Muddle was out of the water? 10 inches

What part of him? his head

◆ STORY 20 How Deep Is the Water?

Only Mr. Muddle's head was out of the water, so his clothes were all wet. "You'd better climb back into the boat," said Ferdie.

"If I do, it might tip over," said Mr. Muddle. "I think I'd better wade back to shore."

"But how will I get back?" asked Ferdie. "I don't know how to row."

"I'll push the boat," Mr. Muddle said, and he gave the boat a push. It glided through the water 3 yards.

"This is fun," said Ferdie, enjoying the ride. "I wonder how far it is back to shore."

Mr. Muddle kept shoving the boat. Every time he shoved the boat, it moved ahead 3 yards. Ferdie counted and discovered that Mr. Muddle had to shove the boat ten times before it got to shore.

Can you figure out how far they were from shore?
30 yards

How far did Mr. Muddle have to push the boat? 30 yards

When they were finally back on land, Mr. Muddle was dripping and shivering. "By the way," said Ferdie, "why did you jump into the water with all your clothes on, Mr. Muddle?"

"I remembered how deep the water is," said Mr. Muddle, "but I forgot how wet it is."

. . . the end

◆ **STORY 20 How Deep Is the Water?**

Story Problems

1 The next time Ferdie and Mr. Muddle went fishing, they caught five fish all together. Ferdie caught five of them.

How many fish did Mr. Muddle catch? zero

But Mr. Muddle did catch four weeds, two tin cans, and an old bicycle tire.

So who caught the most living things? Ferdie

2 Do you know how Ms. Jones gets the toys she sells in her store? She has to buy them. So naturally, she has to sell them for more than she paid. That's how she earns her money. If she buys a toy for $2, she sells it for $3. If she buys a toy for $5, she sells it for $6. If she buys a toy for $1, she sells it for $2.

If Ms. Jones bought a toy for $4, how much would she sell it for? $5

3 "How much is that yo-yo?" asked Ferdie.

"Forty cents," said Ms. Jones. "But because you're such a good customer, I'll sell it to you for half that price."

How much will Ferdie have to pay for the yo-yo? 20¢

"If they're half-price, I'll take two of them," said greedy Ferdie.

How much will he pay for two yo-yos? 40¢

4 The cuckoo clock in the Engs' house goes "Cuckoo" once every hour. One day when the Breezys dropped in to visit, they heard the clock go "Cuckoo" just as they came in the door. The next time the clock went "Cuckoo" was when they were just leaving.

Be careful! Can you figure out how long the Breezys were there? one hour

⑤ Willy has 12¢, Portia has 9¢, and Ferdie has 14¢.

One of them has a dime. Who could it be?
Willy or Ferdie

Could it be Portia? no

Why not? She has less than 10¢.

⑥ Mr. Mudancia used to have 26 teeth in his mouth, but he changed that. He went to the dentist and had two false teeth put in.

How many teeth does he have in his mouth now? 28

⑦ Loretta the Letter Carrier bought a pound of peanuts. She gave 30 peanuts to Liz and 30 peanuts to Ivan.

How many peanuts does she have left? can't tell

What do you need to know? how many peanuts are in a pound

⑧ Marcus ran around the block in four minutes. Manolita ran around in six minutes, and Ferdie did it in five minutes.

Who is fastest? Marcus

⑨ It costs a quarter for a bag of pretzels. "Guess I can't buy any," said Mr. Muddle. "I have only 30 cents."

Is he right? no

Why not? 30¢ is worth more than a quarter.

⑩ Mr. Muddle was going to visit Willy, who lives three blocks away. Mr. Muddle forgot and walked one block past Willy's house. Then he remembered where he was going and walked back to Willy's house.

How far did Mr. Muddle walk all together? five blocks

Thinking Story References

Correlation of the Student Edition Lessons and Thinking Story References